The Last Apostles on Earth

The Last Apostle on Earth

The Last Apostles on Earth

Roger Sapp

Companion Press
P.O. Box 310
Shippensburg, PA 17257-0310

"Good Stewards of the
Manifold Grace of God"

ISBN 1-56043-568-2

For Worldwide Distribution
Printed in the U.S.A.

Acknowledgments

This book is dedicated to the Apostle and High Priest of my confession, Jesus Christ. I must thank Him for those whom He has used in my life to enable me to write the things in this book. My parents, Nelson and Loraine Sapp, were His instruments, encouraging me throughout my life. I thank the Lord for the two years of patience and understanding that my wife Ann and my children showed me as I prepared this manuscript. I am grateful also to the Lord for Dr. Curry N. Vaughan for his confidence in me in my youthful ministry and for imparting a vision of the Church as the prepared Bride of Christ that I will not forget.

Contents

Book One

The Apostle
in the New Testament

Chapter 1

The First Apostles

Apostles Are Often Hidden

Apostles are often hidden. In the English versions of the New Testament, they are sometimes hidden by translation and by simple misunderstanding. In this day God is shining His light on the New Testament to reveal this ministry. Apostles are hidden to those who have been improperly taught about them and therefore do not accurately see them in the New Testament, in Church history, or in modern times. God's light is illuminating the New Testament to a new generation of teachers who are now revealing the ministry of the apostle to those who have "ears to hear" and "eyes to see."

In much the same way as the Messiah was unrecognized among many of His own people as He was growing up, so apostles have been growing up in our midst, hidden and unrecognized by the Church. The Holy Spirit is preparing them in character and power for a special time to come. Apostles have been hidden by God from most eyes until they are ready to be set by Him into their prominent end-time role.

All this previous hiddenness demands a careful and deliberately simple approach to the subject of apostles, with openness to the instruction of the Word of God. Previously formed conceptions can be barriers to new understanding if they are held in too high esteem. "Old wineskins" will not hold the "new wine" that God will pour out on the Church in the last days. Only the Church of His creation and design will be able to contain the presence and power of His Spirit in the last days and be prepared to be the Bride of Christ.

The object of this book, therefore, is to shed some light on the ministry of the apostle as revealed in the Scriptures, thereby helping the Church to make "room once" again for a proper modern expression of this ministry. Hopefully, by the end of this work you will have a definitive answer as to what an apostle is.

Dangers exist in this kind of information for those who are proud, self-willed, and immature. Anyone who would try to apply what is written here without the wisdom and guidance of the Holy Spirit will themselves create more barriers for the restoration of this essential ministry. A carnal, untimely application of the things in this book will do more harm than good. Information devoid of wisdom, patience, and love will not set us free. The Holy Spirit must have full reign as restored truth is applied to our individual situations.

Defining the Word *Apostle*

The word *apostle* is a transliterated word, one that is taken directly or almost directly from another language with little change. In this case, *apostle* is taken from the common Greek word *apostolos*. This word literally means "one sent forth." *Apo* literally means "from," and *stolos* comes from *stello*, which means "I send."[1] Within the New Testament and in other classical Greek literature, *apostolos* has the simple meaning of "one sent as representative of another," the representative deriving his authority and power from the one sending him.[2] This simple definition is the root of the meaning of *apostle*. Although this is the root meaning,

---

1.   pg. 35, The Expanded Vine's Expository Dictionary of New Testament Words.
2.   pg. 348, Duffield.

there must be much more written to reveal the strength and depth of the biblical use of the term. The New Testament provides an abundance of information to reveal this ministry fully.

Apostles Will Become Prominent Again
This ministry was exceedingly important to the establishing of the early Church, and it will be exceedingly important in preparing the Church for the Second Coming of Christ. At the beginning of this age, apostles were the first ministry established. The apostle will also be the last ministry restored and reestablished at this end of the age. Apostles will return to prominence in the Church just before the return of Christ.

The clear emergence of apostles into new prominence will be a great sign of the nearness of the end of the age and Christ's Second Coming. This new prominence will come by way of an apostles' movement within the Church in the closing decades of this age. There are indications that this movement will come soon; the Church will need to be able to sort out the true apostle from the pretender.

This revelation is supported by a historical awareness of what God has done already in this century. It appears that a prophets' movement has taken place throughout the Body of Christ in the last half of the 1980's and early 1990's. There have been mature prophets in this movement who have been predicting a future movement of the Holy Spirit to restore the apostle to his place of prominence and function. Therefore, there is a great need for clarity concerning the apostle and his place in the Church. The importance of understanding the subject of apostles will increase dramatically as the season of this movement draws near.

New Testament the Only Adequate Guide
There will be those who will want to create their own doctrines about the ministry of the apostle outside of what the New Testament reveals about this ministry. There are already books available on apostles that teach readers that the present-day apostle is not

like the first apostles. The Church cannot afford for a less-than-scriptural apostle to be given authority in the Church. Only that which the Scriptures reveal about the apostle is adequate to measure apostolic claims. The Church cannot afford to receive "revelations" and teachings that proclaim an unscriptural message about present-day apostles. It is not our decision to choose what an apostle is; the ministry of the apostle is already abundantly revealed in the Scriptures.

Large Number of References to Apostles

The New Testament reveals in many ways how important this ministry is. The most obvious indication is the large number of references to it throughout the New Testament. In the New International Version of the New Testament, there are 87 references to *apostle*, *apostles*, *apostolic*, or *apostleship*.

This large number of references becomes even more impressive when compared to the fact that the term *evangelist* is only mentioned three times. Surprisingly enough, even the use of the term *shepherd* comes in as only a distant second to *apostle*. In all its forms, *shepherd* is only mentioned 24 times in the New Testament (this includes the one reference to *pastor* found in Ephesians 4:11). Even these 24 references are somewhat misleading because a good number of them do not address the shepherd as a ministry, while all 87 references to *apostle* reveal a ministry to the Church through their context.

Some Apostles Are Hidden by Translation

In addition to the number of direct references to the ministry of the apostle, there are also some indirect references that translators have intentionally or unintentionally disguised through inconsistent translation of the Greek word for *apostle*. In many versions, such as the King James and the New International, the translators have occasionally chosen to use the word *messenger* in place of *apostle*. These inconsistencies may be the reflections of a theology that finds difficulty in accepting the large number of men that the New Testament describes as apostles. Adding to the confusion, the phrase "one who is sent" has been used in several versions of John 13:16 instead of the word *apostle*. Two negative references to apostles are given in the New Testament as well. The first is a reference to "false apostles."[3] The second uses the phrase, "those who claim to be apostles but are not, and [you] have found them false."[4]

The verb forms of this word (such as *apostello*) are normally translated "send" or "sent." Although they are not all used to describe apostolic ministry, they are still used over 100 times,[5] thus making "being sent forth" a very prominent idea to all who read the original Greek manuscripts of the New Testament. It is only possible for English readers of the New Testament to ignore this massive number of references because they are hidden by the translation.

The 12 Disciples Become 12 Apostles

The initial sending of the 12 disciples as apostles can instruct us as to what the Scriptures mean by the term *apostle*. Before the disciples were sent, Jesus conducted His preaching ministry with Kingdom power. The disciples accompanied Him as learners and observers.

Jesus went through all the towns and villages, teaching in their synagogues, preaching the good news of the kingdom and healing every disease and sickness. When He saw the crowds, He had compassion on them, because they were harassed and helpless, like sheep without a shepherd (Matthew 9:35-36).

Jesus reacted in compassion to the needs of the crowds. They were "harassed and helpless" because they were "sheep without a shepherd." The implication here is that a true shepherd should be able to do something about the wretched spiritual condition of the

---

3.   2 Corinthians 11:13.
4.   Revelation 2:2.
5.   pg. 859, *Young's Analytical Concordance.*

people. What then is the solution that Jesus offers His disciples for dealing with the spiritual condition of these people? He tells His disciples to pray for God to "send out" workers into His harvest field.

> *Then He said to His disciples, "The harvest is plentiful but the workers are few. Ask the Lord of the harvest, therefore, to **send out** workers into His harvest field* (Matthew 9:37-38).

The chapter division sometimes hides the connection between these verses and those that follow. (Readers should note that chapter divisions were not in the original manuscripts.) Jesus then calls the 12 disciples and gives them the same authority and supernatural power that He has been exercising. At this point the disciples are called *apostles* for the first time.

> *He called His **twelve disciples** to Him and gave them authority to drive out evil spirits and to heal every disease and sickness. These are the names of the **twelve apostles**: first, Simon (who is called Peter) and his brother Andrew; James son of Zebedee, and his brother John; Philip and Bartholomew; Thomas and Matthew the tax collector; James son of Alphaeus, and Thaddaeus; Simon the Zealot and Judas Iscariot, who betrayed Him* (Matthew 10:1-4).

The meaning of *apostle* is clear in the next verse as Jesus gives them specific instructions when they are *sent out* to minister in the power of the Spirit.

> *These twelve Jesus **sent out** with the following instructions: "Do not go among the Gentiles or enter any town of the Samaritans. Go rather to the lost sheep of Israel. As you go, preach this message: 'The kingdom of heaven is near.' Heal the sick, raise the dead, cleanse those who have leprosy, drive out demons. Freely you have received, freely give* (Matthew 10:5-8).

The commission of the 12 disciples to heal the sick and cast out demons and their being sent forth is what made them apostles. This is expressed in chart form below.

> **Twelve disciples⇒Sent to preach, heal & deliver from evil spirits⇒Twelve apostles**

God's answer to the problem of the "harassed and helpless" sheep of this world is for the Lord of the Harvest to *send out apostles* who will be the *shepherds* to the flock. These sent-forth ones will be able to help the harassed and helpless by the supernatural power of the Holy Spirit in healing, miracles, and deliverance from evil spirits. The 12 Apostles certainly demonstrated this power in their ministries as recorded in the Gospels and later accounts of their exploits supplied by other sources. Without this power, no man can truly be an apostle.

Apostles Are Shepherds

The term *shepherd* is very important in the Scriptures. In this age it is normally associated with the ministry of the pastor. However, in both the Old Testament and New Testament it is given a larger context; it is the picture of spiritual leadership given for the godly. Initially in God's plan, Christ Himself and then His 12 Apostles were the shepherds of God's flock. Later God extended this ministry to others. All God's servants, apostles, and otherwise, should be shepherds and should have the heart of the Good Shepherd. All apostles are shepherds, but not all shepherds are apostles.

The 12 Apostles After the Ascension

The Gospels record a multitude of facts about the 12 Apostles before the Ascension, but next to nothing afterward. The Book of Acts and the letters of Paul give us a little information about a few of them. Most of them, however, are not mentioned by the New Testament after the outpouring of the Holy Spirit recorded in Acts chapter 2. This lack of information can give the false impression that they were unproductive for the Kingdom of God.

Part of this impression comes from the percentage of the New Testament comprised by Paul's letters. Additionally, Luke's documentation of Paul's travels in the last half of the Book of Acts makes it seem that Paul was doing most of the work of the gospel. Since we do not have clear documentation of the lives of the other apostles, we cannot properly compare between Paul and the other apostles.

Most of the information we have about the other apostles comes from individuals who were disciples of the apostles or disciples of their disciples. These individuals have been called the "Early Church Fathers." Many manuscripts and portions of the ancient manuscripts of their writings exist today, tens of thousands of copies. Their writings can be considered slightly more reliable than legend. More credibility can be given to those who lived closer to the first century, but even the writings of these persons do not have the reliability of the New Testament. However, where several of these sources agree independently from one another, this information may be considered seriously.

If we list the 12 Apostles from the other accounts, we find a few variations in the names that are easily resolved through a comparison of the accounts. In that culture, it was possible for a person to have several names due to the various languages in the area. For instance, a Jew might have had Hebrew, Greek, and Latin names. Paul, for instance, also had the Hebrew name Saul.

Generally speaking, there are independent sources concerning the field or geographical location of the later ministry of each of the remaining apostles. This information reveals that they took seriously the command of Jesus to take the gospel to the whole world. Here is a list of the 12 Apostles of the Lamb with their respective areas of ministry in later life. Some of these fields are historically documented, and others are simply strongly suggested by the many legends from these areas about the particular apostles named. Two of the apostles listed did not have the opportunity to minister outside of Israel due to their early deaths.

Apostle	Ministry Field
Andrew	Greece & Black Sea
Bartholomew (Nathaniel)	Armenia (Iran)
James, the Younger	Spain & Britain
James, the Elder	Early martyr
John	Asia Minor
Matthew (Levi)	Northern Africa
Peter (Simon, Cephas)	Jews in the Dispersion
Thaddaeus (Lebbeus, Judas)	Syria
Thomas	India
Philip	Phrygia (Turkey)
Simon	S.E. of Caspian Sea
Judas Iscariot	Died by suicide

Team Ministry Among the Apostles

Lest we think that the apostles were loners in some sense, we need to remind ourselves that among them there were at least four pairs of brothers: Peter and Andrew;[6] James and John;[7] Philip and Bartholomew (sometimes called Nathanael);[8] James and Judas (not Iscariot), and perhaps Matthew.[9] This Judas is called Lebbeus and Thaddaeus as well. According to tradition, Simon the Zealot was a brother of James and Judas, but that is not found in the New Testament.

Some of the traditions have the apostles paired together in teams of two, three, and four. An apocryphal tradition from the second century assigns Peter, Andrew, Matthew, and Bartholomew to their field of the regions north and northwest of Palestine. This would include the regions of Syria, Galatia, Pontus, Scythia, and the coasts of the Black Sea. This tradition assigns to Thaddaeus,

---

6.   Matthew 4:18.
7.   Matthew 4:21.
8.   John 1:43-51
9.   Mark 2:14; Luke 6:16; Acts 1:13.

Thomas, and Simon the Canaanite Zealot the eastern countries of Mesopotamia, Parthia, Edessa, Babylon, and India. The tradition says the field of John and Philip was Asia Minor, including the cities of Ephesus and Heirapolis.[10]

The 12 Apostles Immortalized

The 12 Apostles, minus Judas, will be forever immortalized by their names being placed on the twelve foundations of the New Jerusalem. These twelve are the foundational stones placed in line with the Cornerstone, Jesus.

> *The wall of the city had twelve foundations, and on them were the names of the twelve apostles of the Lamb* (Revelation 21:14).

One of the 12 Apostles was the traitor Judas Iscariot. It is unlikely that his name is on the foundation stones of the New Jerusalem. There is no real scriptural reason to undo what the remaining 11 apostles did shortly after the Ascension of the Lord. In Acts 1, the remaining 11 apostles prayerfully selected the disciple Matthias by lot to replace Judas. Matthias' name is surely on one of these foundation stones. A more complete discussion on Matthias' selection follows in Appendix B and in the next chapter.

The 12 Apostles in the Resurrection

Before His crucifixion and resurrection, the Lord Jesus told His apostles that their future ministry in the coming Kingdom would be kingly. He said they would sit upon thrones and would be doing the kingly work of judging.

> *Jesus said to them, "I tell you the truth, at the renewal of all things, when the Son of Man sits on His glorious throne, you who have followed Me will also sit on **twelve thrones, judging** the twelve tribes of Israel"* (Matthew 19:28; see also Luke 22:30).

---

10.   pg. 200, Vol I., Schaff.

This kingly connection will be explored after we complete our survey of the rest of the New Testament apostles.

Summary of Chapter One

The ministry of the apostle is greatly misunderstood in our day. Since there are indications that God is beginning to restore the ministry of the apostle to its former prominence, it is important for the Church to fully understand this ministry. The New Testament is the only trustworthy guide to rediscovering the ministry of the apostle. The term *apostle* means "sent-forth one." The original 12 Apostles were "sent forth" by the Lord in the power of the Spirit to be shepherds of the flock. They were equipped to deal with the helpless and harassed sheep through healing, miracles, and deliverance from evil spirits. With a couple of notable exceptions, the 12 Apostles were successful after Christ's ascension in continuing to carry out this mission in the nations to which the Lord sent them. The 12 Apostles also have an important future mission after the resurrection—as kings in the age to come.

Chapter 2

The Other Apostles

No Secondhand Apostles

Apostles are often hidden due to the widespread lack of understanding that there were other apostles in addition to the original Twelve. Although a few scholars have noted this, other expressions of modern theology have discounted them in various ways and continued to give the impression that the 12 Apostles are the only true apostles. However, it is clear that the New Testament does not discount apostolic ministry at all. Each of these other apostles was valued by the Church and in some cases became more important in the history of the Church than the original 12 Apostles.

Matthias, the "Replacement Apostle"

In examining the prominence of apostles in the New Testament, we find quite a number of individuals described as apostles. As mentioned in Chapter One, we must add *Matthias* to our list of apostles. The following passage relates that Matthias was chosen from among the disciples of Jesus to replace Judas.

> *So they proposed two men: Joseph called Barsabbas (also known as Justus) and **Matthias**. Then they prayed, "Lord, You know everyone's heart. Show us which of these two You have chosen to take over this apostolic ministry, which*

*Judas left to go where he belongs." Then they cast lots, and the lot fell to **Matthias**; so he was added to the eleven apostles* (Acts 1:23-26).

What happened to Matthias is uncertain, and the sources are scanty and unreliable. However, what they do say is that Matthias ministered in Judea and in Cappadocia, where he was finally martyred. All testimony to him reveals that he was faithful unto his death, which was thought to be about A.D. 61 or 64.[1] If we continue to count Judas as an apostle, then Matthias becomes the thirteenth apostle we have discussed. Further discussion about Matthias can be found in Appendix B.

Paul and Barnabas, Apostles of the Church of Antioch

Paul and *Barnabas* are the fourteenth and fifteenth apostles revealed in the New Testament. They were called while members of the church at Antioch. The passage reveals that they were either prophets and/or teachers prior to their call to be apostles.

*In the Church at Antioch there were prophets and teachers: **Barnabas**, Simeon called Niger, Lucius of Cyrene, Manaen (who had been brought up with Herod the tetrarch) and **Saul**. While they were worshiping the Lord and fasting, the Holy Spirit said, "Set apart for Me **Barnabas and Saul** for the work to which I have called them." So after they had fasted and prayed, they placed their hands on them and **sent** them off. The two of them, **sent** on their way by the Holy Spirit, went down to Seleucia and sailed from there to Cyprus* (Acts 13:1-4).

The tense of the verbs in this statement indicates that this call was already known to Paul ("Saul" in this passage) and Barnabas. The Holy Spirit was simply making it public to the other prophets and teachers who were praying and fasting together. It is not readily apparent from the passage how the Holy Spirit made it known.

---

1.   pg. 254, Lockyer.

However, since the "Holy Spirit said," it is not a large leap in logic to speculate that the spiritual gift of prophecy was manifested through one of the other three individuals present. This revelation of God's living word came as a confirmation of what Paul and Barnabas already knew personally and it was revealed to these three other witnesses.

Paul (Saul) and Barnabas' call as apostles may not be apparent from this passage until we discover that the word *sent* is used twice in the passage. This is a verb form of the word for "apostle." They were *sent* by the Holy Spirit and *sent* by the Antioch church.

After the time of this commissioning Paul and Barnabas are referred to as apostles. The next chapter of Acts provides us with the first reference in which they are identified clearly as apostles. Acts 14:4 refers to both of them being apostles; however, since this verse doesn't actually mention their names, Acts 14:14, which mentions their names, seems more substantial for this point.

*But when the **apostles Barnabas and Paul** heard of this, they tore their clothes and rushed out into the crowd, shouting* (Acts 14:14).

In the last chapter, we looked at how the Lord Jesus sent out His disciples in His authority and power, making them apostles. The same pattern is revealed in this passage through the Spirit of Christ, the Holy Spirit, sending Paul and Barnabas. Based on this sending they become apostles. The chart below expresses this divine idea.

> **5 prophets & teachers⇒The Spirit sends 2 by the other 3⇒apostles Barnabas & Paul**

Sent by the Lord and the Church

This dual "sending" reveals the wisdom of God. No man is an apostle without both kinds of "sending." No man is an apostle without the sending of God—no matter what the Church may think. No man is an apostle without God first revealing his ministry to the Church and then the Church sending him. This does not mean that all churches will acknowledge the call. However, some portion of the Church must acknowledge the call eventually for it to be legitimate and authentic. Every apostolic calling is proven through independent human witnesses given to the Church. This divine balance protects the Church from immature or false apostles.

Barnabas' Call to Apostleship

Paul's call to apostleship is unquestioned by the Church. However, it may be surprising for the average Christian to discover that Barnabas was called as an apostle at the same time as Paul. This passage in Acts is not the only source we have to Barnabas' apostleship. Paul places Barnabas on equal footing with himself in a significant passage in First Corinthians. Here he discusses the right of apostles to be supported by the giving of the Church and to take along a believing wife in the work. Paul says that he and Barnabas have as much right to do so as any *other apostles.*

> *Don't we have the right to take a believing wife along with us, as do the **other apostles** and the Lord's brothers and Cephas? Or is it only **I and Barnabas** who must work for a living?* (1 Corinthians 9:5-6)

A great deal of extra-biblical information exists about Barnabas. Unfortunately, little can be said to be reliable. Some traditions have Barnabas ministering in as far-flung locations as Alexandria and Rome. Some have Barnabas returning to his native Cyprus and dying there. One thing is certain: There is strong testimony to Barnabas being faithful to his God-given ministry as an apostle.

Paul's Call to Apostleship

Paul, in his introduction to the letter to the Galatian church, refers to his call to apostleship, which was made public to the Church in Acts 13. Some have suggested that Paul's call to apostleship came during his conversion experience near Damascus or shortly thereafter while he was blind and helpless. This is possible, yet there is no specific mention of it in the conversion account in Acts 9. In Paul's own description of his conversion in Acts 22:21, he uses a verb form of the word *apostle.* However, Paul is not described by Luke as an apostle until after his association with the church at Antioch some years later. Acts 13 is the first place where a verb form of the word *apostolos* is used in relation to Paul, and he is not referred to as an apostle (noun form) until Acts 14. Finally, no apostolic work is performed by Paul until after Acts 13, which seems to settle the question decisively.

We can perhaps say with relative certainty that the call for apostleship came at conversion, but that its understanding and implications were not revealed at that time. Then sometime prior to the events of Acts chapter 13, the specifics of the call began to become clear. In other words, the seed of apostleship was planted at conversion but did not germinate until Acts 13. The fact that the five men in the Acts 13 passage (including Barnabas and Paul) are described as prophets and teachers and not as apostles until after the sending forth strengthens this further. Paul describes this apostolic "sending" in the first verse of Galatians.

> *Paul, an apostle—sent not from men nor by man, but by Jesus Christ and God the Father, who raised Him from the dead* (Galatians 1:1).

In this passage Paul clearly interprets his call for us—he understood he was being sent divinely and not by the will of the Church. The Church only recognizes by ordination what God has done by the anointing of the Spirit. Unfortunately, some churches seem to believe that their religious ceremonies produce the work of the Holy Spirit. This idea is certainly contrary to Scripture and experience. It leads to unanointed men in ecclesiastical offices in the Church. Further, the Church can confuse a natural giftedness, superior intellect, or organizational ability with evidence of the call of God. This was not the case with Paul. He knew that his natural ability was not the basis of his calling.

Paul as the Pattern Apostle

Paul's deeds are well-documented in the Scriptures since Luke focused the last half of the Book of Acts on him. One might speculate that if Luke had chosen instead to record the travels and deeds of Peter, Barnabas, or any of the other apostles, the Church today might have a different image of Paul and perhaps elevate one of the other apostles. However, since the Holy Spirit, working through His servants in the first century and in the canonization process of the New Testament a few centuries later, has chosen Paul as the primary example of a functioning apostle, we cannot refuse to admire him.

In the Book of Acts Luke gives extensive information about Paul and his travels. Paul also gives us complementary fragments of historical information and personal information about himself through his letters. This information when gathered together enables us to have a fairly clear picture of this man and what he accomplished. However, it is still incomplete since it does not record his last days or death. The Book of Acts finishes with Paul imprisoned in Rome and still alive. We do know from other historical sources that he was martyred in Rome during the reign of the Emperor Nero at about A.D. 68. There is some evidence that Paul was released for another ministry trip after the end of the Book of Acts before he was imprisoned and then beheaded at 63 years of age. Much of what will be said of the apostle in subsequent chapters will be drawn from Scriptures both about and from Paul. Further discussion concerning Paul can be found in Appendix B.

Silas and Timothy, the Companion Apostles

The sixteenth and seventeenth apostles are *Silas* and *Timothy*. These apostles are easy to miss in a cursory reading of the New Testament. Two verses, however, when carefully compared clearly demonstrate that Paul knew them to be apostles. Paul includes Silas and Timothy in the introductory verses of First Thessalonians where he writes:

> *Paul,* **Silas and Timothy,** *To the Church of the Thessalonians in God the Father and the Lord Jesus Christ: Grace and peace to you* (1 Thessalonians 1:1).

A few verses later, Paul describes the three of them as "we," indicating the continued inclusion of Silas and Timothy in his discourse. He refers to the three of them—Silas, Timothy, and himself—as apostles.

*We were not looking for praise from men, not from you or anyone else. As **apostles** of Christ we could have been a burden to you...* (1 Thessalonians 2:6-7).

Silas, the Prophetic Apostle

Silas was one of the "chief men among the brethren."[2] He was a man of some importance and a distinguished member of the council in Jerusalem. This means that he was probably an early disciple of Christ, not a novice trainee under Paul as some would suggest. We also find that in addition to apostleship he held the calling of a prophet as well.[3] Like Paul, he was also a Roman citizen.[4] His Roman name was *Silvanus*. Tradition tells us that Silas was often left behind to do follow-up ministry when Paul when on to the next site of ministry.[5] This is strong testimony to his wisdom and maturity.

Timothy, Paul's "Understudy Apostle"

Timothy was the "understudy apostle." He was a convert of Paul, even though he had a godly mother and grandmother.[6] There is a wealth of information related to Timothy in the New Testament, including two letters from Paul to him. The second of these letters was written while Paul was imprisoned in Nero's dungeon near the end of his life. They instruct and encourage Timothy to continue the work that they had begun together. Many passages of the letter demonstrate the closeness of their relationship. For instance, in several passages Paul addresses Timothy as "my son." It is possible that Paul saw Timothy as his successor in ministry.

As an additional confirmation of Timothy's apostleship, we see Paul giving him specific instructions in First and Second

---

2.   Acts 15:22-27.
3.   Acts 15:30-32.
4.   Acts 16:35-40.
5.   pg. 231, Lockyer.
6.   Acts 16:1; 2 Timothy 1:5.

Timothy that include appointing leadership in the local churches, clearly an apostolic function. In First Timothy 3, we see Paul teaching Timothy about the qualifications of the overseer and deacon. This was to help Timothy in his apostolic function to select men in the local churches who were qualified for these roles. Additionally, we see in Second Timothy Paul's instructions to Timothy to "do the work of an evangelist." This is not to say that Timothy was an evangelist, but rather that the apostle must also evangelize the lost rather than only working in the midst of the Church.

James, the Apostle and the Lord's Brother

The eighteenth apostle is *James*, the brother of Jesus. This is the same apostle who later wrote the book of James in the New Testament and became the spokesman and leader of the church at Jerusalem. Once again Paul is our source regarding this man's apostleship. In describing his trip to Jerusalem to meet with Peter, Paul says he did not meet with any apostles other than Peter and *James*.

> *I saw none of **the other apostles**—only **James**, the Lord's brother* (Galatians 1:19).

Apollos, the Eloquent Apostle

The apostle that we will list as the nineteenth is *Apollos*, the eloquent Alexandrian Jew. Paul, in his correction to the Corinthian church for their disunity, describes Apollos as an apostle. Paul begins this passage with an inclusive statement about "myself and Apollos." Throughout the passage, Paul uses the pronoun "us," referring to himself and Apollos. He then says that the "us" is "us apostles," including himself and Apollos.

> *Now, brothers, I have applied these things to **myself and Apollos** for your benefit...You have become kings—and that without **us**!...For it seems to me that God has put **us apostles** on display at the end of the procession...* (1 Corinthians 4:6,8-9).

Again it seems apparent that Paul thought of Apollos as on a par with himself as an apostle. He makes no distinction between himself and Apollos as apostles. In this passage, Paul also makes the kingly connection with the ministry of the apostle. This connection will be developed later in this book.

Andronicus and Junias, Outstanding Apostles

It doesn't take as careful a reading of the Book of Romans to discover two more apostles by the names of *Andronicus* and *Junias*.

> Greet **Andronicus and Junias**, *my relatives who have been in prison with me. They are outstanding among the **apostles**, and they were in Christ before I was* (Romans 16:7).

These apostles were not only Paul's relatives, but were apparently prison mates as well. It is also significant to our discussion about apostles to discover that these nearly unknown apostles were Christians or even apostles before Paul. The language here inspires another thought: If these relatively unknown apostles were "outstanding" among the apostles, could there be quite a few more unknown apostles who were not as outstanding that the New Testament doesn't mention at all? These two apostles, Andronicus and Junias, bring the total to 21 apostles.

This passage is also the one place in the New Testament that allows for the possibility of a woman being an apostle. However, this possibility is weakened because there is a textual variant involved. A few of the ancient manuscripts use the female form of the name *Junias*, but the majority have the male form. It could be argued that someone who didn't like the idea of female apostles corrupted the original text. However, the textual variant is more likely just an early copying error and there was no intention involved at all. There is no support elsewhere in the New Testament for a woman to be an apostle.

Epaphroditus, the Apostle From Philippi

The twenty-second apostle is *Epaphroditus*, the apostle who was ill before Paul wrote about him. Paul describes this apostle in his letter to the church at Philippi. It is easy to miss this reference; it is hidden by translation. This passage is one of the places where the New International Version translators have been inconsistent. They translated the same Greek word in this passage as "messenger" that they translated as "apostle" elsewhere.

> *But I think it is necessary to send back to you **Epaphroditus**, my brother, fellow worker and fellow soldier, who is also your **messenger** [apostle], whom you sent to take care of my needs. For he longs for all of you and is distressed because you heard he was ill* (Philippians 2:25-26).

At Least Two Unnamed Apostles

Another passage hides the twenty-third and twenty-fourth apostles behind the same sort of translation obscuration. It is found in Second Corinthians 8:23. A further inconsistency in translation arises in this case because the translators have chosen the word *representatives* over *apostles* or *messengers* in translating the plural of *apostolos*.

> *As for Titus, he is my partner and fellow worker among you; as for our **brothers**, they are **representatives** [apostles] of the churches and an honor to Christ* (2 Corinthians 8:23).

This problem of translation does not obscure the fact that Paul describes these "brothers" as apostles. While we are not sure about their names or how many apostles these "brothers" amount to, we must conclude that there were at least two.

At Least 12 Post-Ascension Apostles

At this point, it is apparent that at least another 12 apostles have been discovered, all of which were called as apostles after the ascension of Christ into Heaven. In other words, there are as many apostles revealed by the Scriptures to have been called through the work of the Holy Spirit after the Ascension of Christ as there were before who were called directly by Jesus.

Paul indicates to us that the ministry of the apostle, while begun by Christ before the Ascension, continues after the Ascension like the other ministries. Paul reveals in Ephesians that Christ gave ministry gifts to men *after His Ascension.* He starts his list with apostles:

> *But to each one of us* **grace has been given** *as Christ apportioned it. This is why it says:* **"When He ascended on high,** *He led captives in His train and* **gave gifts to men."** *... It was* **He who gave some to be apostles, some to be prophets, some to be evangelists, and some to be pastors and teachers** (Ephesians 4:7-8,11).

A logical conclusion based on this Scripture and others is that if other ministry functions or gifts have been apparent in the various centuries of the Church age, there is no reason to doubt that the ministry gift of the apostle has also been functioning. If there have been pastors throughout the Church age, then it is reasonable to expect that there have been apostles as well.

These ministries have not necessarily taken the title of apostle or even been clearly seen to be apostles by others, but have had the characteristics and anointing, and have done the work of the apostle. It may be that some of the great Christian leaders of the past, have been apostles in times when this ministry was misunderstood and unappreciated even by the apostles themselves.

Jesus, the Ultimate Apostle

This list of apostles must be concluded with the pattern for all ministries, the Lord Jesus Christ Himself. The first and last Apostle is the *Lord Jesus Christ.* All apostles are a gift ministry from Him and reflect Him. All apostles, past, present, and future, must fix their thoughts on Him as *The Apostle.*

> *Therefore, holy brothers, who share in the heavenly calling, fix your thoughts on* **Jesus, the apostle** *and high priest whom we confess* (Hebrews 3:1).

Summary of Chapter Two

In addition to the original 12 Apostles, the New Testament describes at least 12 more apostles, although some of these are hidden by inconsistent translation in English versions of the New Testament. In the case of these post-Ascension apostles, the Holy Spirit sent them in the same way the Lord Jesus sent the original 12. The New Testament writings of Paul, one of these post-Ascension apostles, reveal most of these other apostles. Paul acknowledged these others to have the same ministry as himself and the original 12. Paul also becomes the pattern (not forgetting the Lord Jesus Himself) for all present-day apostles by virtue of the mass of New Testament information from him about himself and the other apostles. Paul's writings and Luke's account of Paul in the Book of Acts give us substantial information that reveals the work of apostolic ministry.

Chapter 3

Identifying Apostolic Ministry

Apostles Must Be Tested

How are apostles to be distinguished from other ministries? This is an important consideration for a number of reasons. First, there will be those who would falsely claim this ministry for themselves and cause havoc among the uninformed of the Church. Second, there will be those called to this ministry who are not yet prepared to assume the role. To avoid damaging these developing immature apostles and the Church, these ministries will need to test their maturity before the Lord to avoid presumption and impatience. Third, there will also be those who are ready to assume their place in service, and the Church must be able to recognize these mature ministries.

If we cannot test properly those who claim this ministry, then its restoration will be painful to the Body of Christ. Consider the words of the risen Christ to one of the seven churches in Asia, praising them for testing those who claim the ministry of the apostle:

> *I know your deeds, your hard work and your perseverance.*
> *I know that you cannot tolerate wicked men, **that you have**
> **tested those who claim to be apostles but are not, and**
> **have found them false*** (Revelation 2:2).

The following five characteristics and apostolic functions reveal and test this ministry, separating it from the other ministries. Each characteristic is important in discerning between a true apostle, an immature apostle, or a false one. The person who claims this ministry must be willing to be tested according to God's Word. He may be a developing apostle, not yet ready to be revealed. Knowing the characteristics may encourage such a one not to prematurely reveal his calling and to be patient and allow God to finish His work in him. This will prevent much pain and trauma to him and the Church through giving authority to an immature apostle.

The Mark of the Apostle: Signs, Wonders and Miracles

The New International Version of the New Testament quotes the apostle Paul's defense of his apostolic ministry and reveals one of the most important qualifications for such ministry. This first qualification is evidenced by powerful manifestations of the Holy Spirit: signs, wonders, and miracles.

*The things that **mark** an apostle—**signs, wonders and miracles**—were done among you with great perseverance* (2 Corinthians 12:12).

One of the things that will separate the ministry of the apostle from other ministries is that it is marked by signs, wonders, and miracles. The initial sending of Jesus' 12 disciples included the commission to heal the sick and cast out evil spirits. There must be this kind of supernatural attestation to the Word of God in the ministry of the apostle. God's love must be manifested along with power to change the lives of the "harassed and helpless." The apostle must be able to heal the sick and to cast out demons as a regular and often-occurring expression of his ministry.

No servant of God can truly claim to be an apostle without the regular occurrence of this supernatural mark in his ministry. This mark of the apostle is one of the primary characteristics that distinguishes the apostle from other ministries. While the apostle is not the only ministry that produces signs, wonders, and miracles, a claim of apostolic ministry is certainly put to the test by this mark.

First Corinthians 12:28 describes a ministry of miracles and healing that is listed separately from the ministry of the apostle. Signs, wonders, and miracles alone are not sufficient to adequately test a claim to apostleship, but their absence will certainly reveal that the ministry being evaluated is not apostolic. No ministry of church planting, no gifted pulpit personality, no eloquent speaker, no leader of many other ministries, no "bishop" can claim the ministry of the apostle without an ongoing ministry of signs, wonders, and miracles. This mark effectively eliminates the claims of many pretenders to this ministry and should make the immature apostle seek God for a greater witness of His grace in power. If he is an apostle, it will eventually be known with a witness of power in miracles, healing, and deliverance from evil spirits as a primary characteristic.

This mark of the apostle as recorded by the Gospels was apparent in the ministry of the original 12 disciples after Jesus sent and commissioned them to heal and deliver. It remained apparent after Jesus' Ascension and after Pentecost.

*"What are we going to do with these men?" they asked. "Everybody living in Jerusalem knows they have done an **outstanding miracle**, and we cannot deny it"* (Acts 4:16).

The preaching of the apostle must be accompanied by deliverance from evil spirits, healing the sick, and miracles. Without this mark, no minister should be considered an apostle. This is the outstanding feature of apostolic ministry that holds the attention of the minds of the public and enables apostles to plant churches rapidly. The Book of Acts records this mark in the ministry of Peter and the other apostles.

*Crowds gathered also from the towns around Jerusalem, bringing their **sick** and those **tormented by evil spirits**, and **all of them were healed** (Acts 5:16).*

We find this mark very present in the later ministry of Paul. Paul relates that His preaching of the gospel was to be accompanied by these works of the Holy Spirit.

My message and my preaching were not with wise and persuasive words, but with a demonstration of the Spirit's power, so that your faith might not rest on men's wisdom, but on God's power (1 Corinthians 2:4-5).

It is apparent from the testimony found in the Book of Acts that Paul's preaching was certainly accompanied by miracles. In fact, God granted not only ordinary miracles, but extraordinary ones.

*God did **extraordinary miracles** through Paul* (Acts 19:11).

These miracles were extraordinary in that they were done at a distance from Paul's person. In the synoptic Gospels, a few miracles of this type were done by Jesus. That is, they were done at a distance. In those cases, Jesus praised the extraordinary faith of those who believed He could accomplish these works of power at a distance. Apparently, the "ordinary" miracles were done in person. It is certainly expected that "ordinary" miracles will be found in the ministry of the apostle.

It is important to reiterate that this mark is not enough to objectively establish that a particular servant of God is an apostle. All servants of God should have occasional signs following their preaching. First Corinthians 12 gives a long list of ministries and also includes those that have ministries of miracles and healings. The true evangelist should also have miracles as a normal part of his service to God and the Church—as demonstrated by Philip, the pattern evangelist. Clearly this mark is not enough to establish the apostleship of a particular servant of God, but it is the first characteristic that every apostolic ministry will have. This mark must also be accompanied by the other characteristics that we find in the New Testament.

Revelation of the Calling to Independent Witnesses

When an apostle is prepared to function in this calling, God will reveal this to independent witnesses. This is the second qualification, and it follows a well-established principle of the Scriptures. Every divine fact that the Lord wishes to establish to the Church is validated on the basis of two or three independent witnesses.[1]

The public calling of Paul and Barnabas to the ministry of apostleship in the opening verses of Acts 13 illustrates the principle of independent witnesses. It is clear from the language of the passage that Paul and Barnabas already knew of their calling as apostles.

> *In the church at Antioch there were prophets and teachers:*
> ***Barnabas***, *Simeon called Niger, Lucius of Cyrene, Manaen (who had been brought up with Herod the tetrarch) and* ***Saul***. *While they were worshiping the Lord and fasting, the Holy Spirit said, "Set apart for Me* ***Barnabas and Saul*** *for the work to which I have called them"* (Acts 13:1-2).

The Holy Spirit said to the other three men present that He had called Paul and Barnabas to the work of the apostle. It is apparent that Paul and Barnabas already knew about their calling. The Holy Spirit said, "*I have called them.*" The tense of the verb indicates that at some previous time, the Holy Spirit had shown Paul and Barnabas their calling as apostles. However, in the right timing, the Holy Spirit revealed this fact to other witnesses, who in turn revealed it to the Church.

Short-Circuiting the Process

The man with the undeveloped apostolic calling must not short-circuit the process by being impatient and trying to install himself as an apostle. Should he begin to announce his calling on

---

1.   Deuteronomy 19:15; Matthew 18:16; 2 Corinthians 13:1; Hebrews 10:25; Revelation 11:3.

his own, he will not have the spiritual credentials of the independent witnesses that God will give him. God will reveal his calling to other fivefold ministries and give them to him as fellow workers and witnesses to his calling.

God will particularly give prophets to the apostle as witnesses. They will come to him by revelation. They will witness to others of their revelation and dedicate themselves to serving the Lord beside him in ministry as God reveals. This can be either on a permanent or temporary basis. No apostle has the right to hold on to those whom God is sending elsewhere. God may send His prophets to be witnesses then send them elsewhere. The apostle should expect a continuing revelation of his calling to others if he is humble and does not short-circuit the Holy Spirit's ministry. It is God's place, not his, to reveal him as an apostle.

The apostle must not resort to fleshly methods of proving his calling to others. He must avoid taking the title of "apostle" early in his ministry, since it too will short-circuit God's work in this area. This is exactly opposite of the way many ministers think they must act in order to accomplish their ministries. They feel that they must advertise and help others find out about their abilities. The true apostle must patiently let God witness to the proper persons, who in turn will obediently witness to others of his calling. Should this take longer than he expects, he should acknowledge that it is for his own good. Nothing of real value will be lost in waiting upon the Lord.

Apostles Know That They Are Apostles

There are those who seem to have the characteristics and functions of an apostle, yet deny the call. We must assume that an individual who refuses to acknowledge his ministry as an apostle is either practicing false humility or must not be an apostle in spite of appearances. We see no false humility on the part of Paul or others about being apostles. Paul's statements about his apostolic call in his letters were written after years of walking in the power of the Spirit. Therefore, it seems wise to be guarded about advertising an apostolic calling when the apostle has only a few of the characteristics operating.

Ministers Are Given to Apostles

The third qualification and characteristic is one of the easiest characteristics to identify in the apostolic ministry. God gives apostles other ministers to work with them in team ministry under their authority. This happens often by revelation to these other ministers as mentioned above. God will reveal the apostle to them and call them to associate themselves with him. The apostle who does not employ the people whom God is giving him into his ministry eventually will lose them to others. The apostle who is a loner and stays alone in ministry is no apostle at all. This passage from Acts illustrates the team ministry of Paul.

*He was accompanied by **Sopater** son of Pyrrhus from Berea, **Aristarchus** and **Secundus** from Thessalonica, **Gaius** from Derbe, **Timothy** also, and **Tychicus** and **Trophimus** from the province of Asia. These men went on ahead and waited for **us** [Luke] at Troas (Acts 20:4-5).*

There are many other passages that indicate this characteristic of apostolic ministry.

*He sent two of his helpers, **Timothy** and **Erastus**, to Macedonia, while he stayed in the province of Asia a little longer (Acts 19:22).*

We know more about Timothy and are thankful that Paul trained him to continue after his death. There are numerous examples in the Scriptures of those who were his close associates, such as Timothy and Silas.

*The brothers immediately sent Paul to the coast, but **Silas** and **Timothy** stayed at Berea. The men who escorted Paul brought him to Athens and then left with instructions for **Silas** and **Timothy** to join him as soon as possible (Acts 17:14-15).*

Wherever you find this ministry, you should find individuals like Timothy and others whom God is discipling in ministry by means of the apostle. The apostle will always have individuals God has given to him to train. He will have young prophets, teachers, evangelists, and pastors to encourage and prepare for greater ministry than his own. God will call some of them into apostolic ministry as well. How greatly God used the men who traveled with Paul and were trained by him is not recorded by history. However, having Paul as an example must have greatly impacted men such as Gaius and Aristarchus.

> *Soon the whole city was in an uproar. The people seized **Gaius** and **Aristarchus**, Paul's traveling companions from Macedonia, and rushed as one man into the theater* (Acts 19:29).

Lest we underestimate the numbers of people closely associated with Paul in ministry, we should explore the end of the Book of Romans for his friends and companions in ministry. We note his pastoral love for these whom God had given him to encourage in the Lord. A few of these friends and ministry associates of Paul are mentioned here from Romans 16.

> ***Timothy**, my fellow worker, sends his greetings to you, as do **Lucius**, **Jason**, and **Sosipater**, my relatives. I, **Tertius**, who wrote down this letter, greet you in the Lord. **Gaius**, whose hospitality I and the whole church here enjoy, sends you his greetings. **Erastus**, who is the city's director of public works, and our brother **Quartus** send you their greetings* (Romans 16:21-23).

Seal of Apostleship: Fully Functioning Churches
The seal of apostleship—coupled with the three characteristics and qualifications above—puts the immature apostle and the pretender to apostleship apart from the true manifestation of this gift.

Even though I may not be an apostle to others, surely I am to you! **For you are the seal** *of my apostleship in the Lord* (1 Corinthians 9:2).

While an individual may have the calling of an apostle, the Church at large should not recognize or honor him as an apostle until he has the *seal of apostleship*. This seal is to have fully functioning churches under his authority. These churches will be ruled by elders appointed by the apostle who continue to recognize his authority even as he proceeds to plant other churches in other locations. This is the fourth qualification and distinguishing characteristic of the apostolic ministry.

Church Planters Are Not Always Apostles

There are many persons who pioneer a church apparently successfully and with God's grace. This does not necessarily make them apostles. However, repeated success in church planting, coupled with the other characteristics above, certainly gives evidence of an apostolic call. Obviously, the greater number of churches recognizing the apostle as an apostle, the more clear the seal is. But this alone does not make the apostle an apostle. He must also have been sent by God, have the mark of miracles and have independent witnesses to his call.

Paul defended his apostleship to the church at Corinth by reminding them of the historic fact of his planting of that particular church. The very fact of their flourishing and growth was testimony of his apostleship. Paul, of course, could have reminded them of the other churches that he planted by the supernatural grace of God. In other words, the apostle starts small and is received by a few churches as their apostle before he is recognized on a larger scale. He must first be tested by his success and fruit on a small scale before the Church at large recognizes him.

Essentially, God's testimony to the truth of the gospel through the ministry of miracles, signs, and wonders enabled Paul to plant churches. The other characteristics of his apostleship, like God's gift to him of other men and women to serve with him, enabled him to continue to exercise apostolic authority through them over the churches he planted.

While church planting is not the focus of this book, most modern works on the subject neglect any discussion of the role of the apostle. Most books on church planting rely on research methods to determine the needs in a particular area, knowledge of ministry team building, and other practical concerns. Although this information is of value, it cannot replace knowledge of God's will and purpose for apostolic ministry. The very absence of information about apostles in these works speaks volumes about the present immaturity of the Church and its lack of serious consideration of the Scriptures.

Church growth information must be modified in the future to address the apostolic role as God further clarifies and reestablishes it. To neglect this scriptural information will produce church planters who will oppose God's apostles in a particular geographical area. Eventually God will cease to wink at our ignorance of this area of ministry. Presently functioning apostles will need to prayerfully reevaluate whether or not God has called them to plant churches in other apostles' fields without consultation with those apostles. The Lord will make serious readjustment in evangelistic and church planting methods as we near the end of the age.

The apostle must eventually take his place in leadership, and all true ministry must relate to him in a given area. He must relate to other apostles to produce a practical unity of the faith. In this the apostles will lead the local churches to war successfully against the evil principalities and powers operating in the localities of their callings. We will elaborate further on spiritual warfare and this practical unity in subsequent chapters.

Serious Resistance from Evil Prince Angels

The fifth characteristic of apostolic ministry is easily overlooked and misunderstood by the Church. The Church seems to believe that ministries that are unopposed and accepted must be blessed, and that ministries that are opposed by others must have something wrong with them. Quite the contrary is true. Those ministries that lead the way in power and renewal will also find great opposition from the enemy. Apostolic ministry can be identified by the amount of opposition it receives. Given the fulfillment of the previous four characteristics listed, how can we not expect serious demonic warfare against the apostle himself?

The apostle seeking to fulfill his ministry calling will encounter very serious demonic opposition in different forms. Indeed, the enemy will seek to overwhelm the apostle before he even gets started. Nevertheless, the apostle will be given all he needs to defend himself and those associated with him. He will successfully bring the battle back to the enemy. He must not yield to self-pity or retaliate in the flesh toward demon-inspired human resistance. He must not develop a persecution complex or use it to justify his own mistakes. Instead, he must develop genuine humility, but without denying his own gifting.

The apostle must be experienced in personal spiritual warfare. He must be able to apply it to himself and his family or he will be defeated before he starts. Attacks may come in a variety of ways: sickness, financial difficulties, marital or family problems. He can be sure that the enemy is aware of him, even if the Church is not. He must be able to apply God's Word and bring the victory of Jesus Christ to his own situation. Even when he has won over these initial challenges to his home life and ministry, he will find the battle has just begun. The apostle will be in continuous spiritual warfare throughout his life.

Demonic Accusation Against Apostles

Serious attacks will come in the form of accusations. This tactic is used against all God's servants, and particularly the apostle. If the enemy can get the church to believe his lies about an apostle, then he can also prevent the local church from becoming what it should be.

The enemy has been extremely successful at his attempts at slander in America. The Church will quickly believe lies about some of God's most powerful servants. The media merely says it, and the Church accepts the accusation as the truth. This will not be the situation in the future. The Church will come to expect this kind of warfare against God's servants. We must remember that in Greek the term *devil* means "the slanderer," and in Hebrew the name *Satan* means "the accuser" or "the opposer." Until the Church recognizes accusation as a demonic attack on the godly, she will continue to suffer defeats to the enemy.

Accusation is the primary weapon the enemy uses against the apostle. The source of the accusation is not human; it is the prince spirit over the field the apostle has been sent to. Paul suffered a great deal of this type of attack upon his ministry. Wherever he went, a fallen angel, "a messenger of Satan," stirred up trouble against him.

> *To keep me from becoming conceited because of these sur-*
> *passingly great revelations, there was given me a **thorn in***
> *my flesh, **a messenger of Satan**, to torment me* (2 Corin-
> thians 12:7).

The translation of the word *messenger* here is inconsistent with its normal translation elsewhere in the New Testament. The Greek word used here is normally transliterated as "angel." In other words, the "thorn in the flesh" is "an angel of Satan."

Paul's thorn in the flesh is thought by some to be some sort of sickness. There is little convincing scriptural evidence for this view. The only real way to determine exactly what this thorn was is to look at how the Greek word is used in the rest of the Bible. The problem with this is that this particular Greek word *skolop* is not used again in the New Testament. However, this Greek word is used in the Greek Old Testament, the Septuagint. There is a great deal of evidence to believe that Paul and other Christian preachers to the Gentiles preached from this version and were there-fore very familiar with it. This also provides the best understanding of this particular Greek word; skolop is used in three places in the Septuagint—Numbers 33:55; Ezekiel 28:24; Hosea 2:6.

In Numbers it is used in reference to those enemies of Israel that the Israelites failed to drive out of the land. It states that these enemies would continue to vex and persecute them. In Ezekiel the word is used similarly. In this context God judges Sidon by declar-ing that they and other enemies of Israel will be no more a "thorn"

① Paul's thorn, the author is in exact agreement with the teaching of Rhema Bible Training Center on this controversial subject.

Identifying Apostolic Ministry   39

to them. In Hosea the usage is not as clear as the previous two. It simply says God will prevent Israel from going after false lovers by a "hedge of thorns." Clearly, none of these three usages of *skolop* relate in any way to physical sickness or distress. Two of the three clearly relate to persecution from enemies. This certainly fits with the idea of the thorn being an angel of Satan.

① The "thorn" strongly appears to be relating to opposition and persecution from enemies stirred up by this satanic angel. This was certainly true in Paul's experience. He suffered many persecutions and almost continuous opposition, particularly from the Jews. The entire context of the passage supports this contention.

The context of Second Corinthians 12:7 says that God allowed this thorn[2] in order to balance the great revelations that Paul was given. The thorn kept him from becoming proud. In other words, although he had a ministry with important divine revelation to impart, this revelation served to increase opposition to his ministry rather than decrease it. This will be true of any modern apostle. The greater the revelation, the greater the opposition from evil princely angels.

Today's apostle must ensure that his lifestyle does not add fuel to the fire. Accusations will come, but he must ensure that they will be false. Trouble from religious people, even from within the churches he plants, will be part of his experience just as it was in Paul's. However, God will give the victory as the apostle patiently stands his ground and prays for wisdom and deliverance. The enemy will provoke the envy of local religious leaders to challenge the apostle. This may be painful, but he must not falter; rather he must continue to battle in love on their behalf for victory over their common enemy.

The apostle cannot afford to be "thin-skinned," or he will find himself battling in the flesh. He must consider accusation as a back-handed compliment from the devil and a spiritual validation of his ministry. If he is patient, he will see opposing leaders return

---

2.   pg. 1142-1143, Vine.

to him years later in brokenness. If he is wise and wins the battle in prayer against the spirits that motivate them, he will gain life-long friends and associates in ministry. Spiritual warfare is an important characteristic of the apostle and will be elaborated upon in greater detail later.

Summary of Chapter Three

The Church must be willing to test apostolic claims. There are identifiable features of the apostolic ministry. The first mark of the apostle is *supernatural attestation.* Regular miracles, signs, and wonders—including casting out evil spirits—are to be expected in apostolic ministry. The second feature is *independent witnesses* to whom God has revealed the apostolic calling. In His timing God will establish the divine truth of an individual's apostleship to the Church. The third feature is *team ministry.* God will give teachers, prophets, pastors, evangelists, and other apostles to the mature apostle to serve with him under his authority. The fourth feature is the seal of apostleship, which is the fruit of *fully functioning churches* under the apostle's authority. The apostle may plant them personally or they may come under his authority by revelation. Lastly, the fifth feature of apostolic ministry is *serious resistance* from evil prince angels which will manifest primarily through accusation or persecution. Some of this will come through religious people motivated by the enemy. God will give grace to overcome all such resistance to the true apostle. These five scriptural characteristics of apostolic ministry give the Church a way of measuring claims of apostleship.

Chapter 4

The Apostle and the Shepherd's Heart

Jesus Is the Chief Shepherd of the Sheep

The Scriptures reveal the Lord Jesus Christ as a shepherd, and all godly shepherds submit to Him. The apostle Peter provides us with two passages telling us about the ministry of Jesus, the Chief Shepherd.

In Scripture the ministry of the shepherd is connected to the ministry of the overseer or elder. This is revealed in the Book of First Peter: ①

*For you were like sheep going astray, but now you have returned to the **Shepherd** and **Overseer** of your souls* (1 Peter 2:25).

Later in this letter Peter reveals Jesus as the *Chief Shepherd.* He connects this high office to His giving of a symbol of authority, the crown, to believers.

*And when the **Chief Shepherd** appears, you will receive the **crown** of glory that will never fade away* (1 Peter 5:4).

The following passage reveals the Lamb, Jesus Christ, upon His throne. Since thrones are for kings, it would not be unusual for the passage to tell us that Jesus is the King. However, it is interesting (but not surprising) that the passage instead tells us that the Lamb is our Shepherd.

> *For the **Lamb at the center of the throne will be their shepherd**; He will lead them to springs of living water. And God will wipe away every tear from their eyes* (Revelation 7:17).

Godly "Rulers" Are Shepherds

Numerous verses throughout the Bible substantiate the clear connection between godly leadership and the shepherd. Consider this Messianic prophecy quoted in Matthew's Gospel that reveals God's rulers as shepherds:

> *But you, Bethlehem, in the land of Judah, are by no means least among the rulers of Judah; for out of you will come a **ruler** who will be the **shepherd** of My people Israel* (Matthew 2:6).

Another example of this truth is found in Revelation. There the translators of the New International Version have even translated the Greek word that means "to shepherd" as *rule*.

> *She gave birth to a son, a male child, who will **rule** [shepherd] all the nations with an iron scepter. And her child was snatched up to God and to His throne* (Revelation 12:5).

The New Testament describes the activity of the Lord Jesus Christ, our Shepherd, as ruling. Not only does the New Testament teach this truth concerning the Lord Jesus, but also of those who believe in Him. The Lord Himself says that the person who overcomes and does His (Christ's) will to the end will be given authority to rule.

> *To him who **overcomes** and **does My will to the end**, I will give **authority over the nations**—He will **rule** [shepherd] them with an iron scepter...* (Revelation 2:26-27)

In this case, as in the previous passage, the New International Version translators have rendered the Greek word for "shepherd" as *rule*.

The 12 Apostles Were Shepherds

As discussed in Chapter One, the Lord Jesus Christ sent the first 12 Apostles to be *shepherds* of the flock. The shepherd is the scriptural picture of godly leadership. Chapter One related that all apostles are shepherds, but not all shepherds are apostles. Therefore, understanding the nature of the shepherd in the Scriptures is important to our discussion on apostles.

As related in Chapter One, the Lord Jesus Christ sent subordinate shepherd-apostles into the earth to care for His "harassed and helpless" sheep.

When He saw the crowds, He had compassion on them, because they were **harassed and helpless, like sheep without a shepherd** (Matthew 9:36).

In the next few verses of this passage the Lord, out of His compassion, sent out the 12 disciples to these "sheep." They were sent in the healing power of the Holy Spirit to the harassed and helpless. As a result of this sending, the 12 disciples became the 12 Apostles.

It is clear that apostles are sent with the Lord's intent for them to care for others. Any "apostle" who does not have this attitude of humble service in the midst of the flock is no apostle at all. The Scripture speaks to this kind of "shepherd."

*These men are blemishes at your love feasts, eating with you without the slightest qualm—***shepherds who feed only themselves***. They are clouds without rain, blown along by the wind; autumn trees, without fruit and uprooted—twice dead* (Jude 12).

A shepherd who only feeds himself violates Christ's intention for shepherds. He is a "cloud without rain." In other words, he doesn't have the heart of a true shepherd. He is without fruit. This so-called shepherd is not producing the fruit of a true shepherd. That shepherd is "uprooted," meaning that he is not connected with the source of life; therefore, he can only minister death.

Christ Rules Through Shepherds

Although Christ rules individuals through the agency of the Holy Spirit, it is apparent that another powerful expression of the authority of the Kingdom of God is expressed through godly men appointed as subordinate shepherds of the flock. The first shepherds of the flock are apostles. All fivefold ministers are shepherds to the flock, particularly the men who are appointed to local church ministry. These men are generally called *elders* or *overseers*. They are appointed by apostles and are under the apostle's authority. Apostles and elders are likewise under the authority of the Lord Jesus Christ.

The direct relationship between these various terms for leadership is revealed in a passage in the Book of Acts in which Paul speaks to the elders he had appointed in Ephesus. He also calls them overseers. Paul tells them to keep watch over the flock. Elders who are overseers are to shepherd the flock.

*From Miletus, Paul sent to Ephesus for the **elders** of the church...he said to them: "...**Keep watch** over yourselves and all the **flock** of which the Holy Spirit has made you **overseers**. Be **shepherds** of the church of God, which He bought with His own blood"* (Acts 20:17-18,28).

This context demonstrates one of the primary expectations of the godly shepherd, which certainly includes the apostle. He must protect the flock from wolves. The godly shepherd must protect the flock from those who would like to prey upon them. The wolf is the scriptural picture of the false prophet.[1] The false prophet does not care for the sheep, but is out to use and abuse them for his own purposes.

---

1.   Matthew 7:15, 10:16; Luke 10:3; John 10:12; Acts 20:29.

It is clear that the terms *elder, overseer*, and *shepherd* are equivalent terms in this passage. Here they refer to local church ministry. Paul is not the only apostle who tells us of the relationship between these terms. Peter also wrote to encourage these subordinate shepherds, or overseers, to protect themselves from wrong motives such as serving for money. The proper shepherd is to serve the flock willingly, to please the Lord, and not because of the financial rewards.

> Be **shepherds** of God's flock that is under your care, serving as **overseers**—not because you must, but because you are willing, as God wants you to be; not greedy for money, but eager to serve (1 Peter 5:2).

(In the King James Version *overseer* is translated "bishop," which causes some confusion. For a full discussion of the term *bishop*, see Appendix A.)

The Functions of Shepherds

The Book of Ezekiel gives us a considerable amount of information about the functions of the godly shepherd. Everything here applies to the apostolic ministry, although the passage itself is a prophecy against ungodly shepherds. God is speaking correction to them about their failures as shepherds. In spite of the negative tone in this passage, we can draw from it positive truths about shepherds. Here are the words of God to the shepherds of Israel.

> The word of the Lord came to me: "Son of man, prophesy against the shepherds of Israel; prophesy and say to them: 'This is what the Sovereign Lord says: Woe to the shepherds of Israel who **only take care of themselves**! Should not shepherds **take care of the flock**?" (Ezekiel 34:1-2)

The first of the truths we can draw from this passage is that godly shepherds should *take care of the flock* and *not themselves*. In the Gospel of John the Lord Jesus reveals that the true shepherd "lays down his life for the sheep." However, these shepherds were

living selfishly. God's correction of them continues in the next
verse of Ezekiel:

> *You eat the curds, clothe yourselves with the wool and
> slaughter the choice animals, but **you do not take care of
> the flock.** You have not **strengthened the weak** or **healed
> the sick** or **bound up the injured.** You have not **brought
> back the strays** or **searched for the lost.** You have **ruled
> them harshly and brutally** (Ezekiel 34:3-4).*

The compassion of God for His flock is apparent in this passage. The apostle and all other shepherds must have the heart of
the Good Shepherd. In these verses God tells us what He means by
"taking care of the flock." A godly shepherd strengthens the weak,
heals the sick, binds up the injured, brings back the strays, and
searches for the lost. The rule of the godly shepherd is not harsh or
brutal. The godly shepherd does not dominate the flock. This passage reveals God's grief over the scattering and destruction of His
flock for the lack of good shepherds.

Christ Is the Good Shepherd

Christ Himself has the positive qualities this passage describes
for a shepherd. He lived to fulfill His Father's expectations of a
good shepherd, and referred to Himself as such.

> *I am the good shepherd. The good shepherd lays down His
> life for the sheep* (John 10:11).

Christ is the good Shepherd because He willingly laid down
His life for the sheep. Christ not only lived for the sheep; He also
died for them. The good shepherds whom He has called to Himself
also live sacrificially for the sheep. They daily lay down their
lives. The man who is called as an apostle must be willing to sacrifice for the sake of the flock. If he is unwilling to do so, he lacks
the heart of a shepherd. He disqualifies himself from being a good
shepherd and qualifies himself as a hired hand instead.

The hired hand is not the shepherd who owns the sheep. So when he sees the wolf coming, he abandons the sheep and runs away. Then the wolf attacks the flock and scatters it. The man runs away because he is a hired hand and cares nothing for the sheep (John 10:12-13).

God has not given His sheep to the hired hand. His sheep belong to true and good shepherds. The hired hand is unwilling to face any real pressure concerning the flock. He is unwilling to fight for the sheep against the wolf that seeks to devour them. He will abandon the sheep if he perceives it to be in his best interest. His real interest is in money and he does not really care for the sheep. On the other hand, the good shepherd cannot be bought. He does not serve for money. He serves the Lord by serving His flock and entrusts his finances to God. The true apostle is a true and good shepherd.

Summary of Chapter Four

The Bible, both Old and New Testaments, portrays the shepherd as the picture of godly leadership. In the Bible the terms *rule* and *shepherd* are often related. The Lord Jesus Christ is revealed as the Good and Chief Shepherd. His ruling authority over each believer is expressed through the Word of God, the Holy Spirit and through appointed shepherds. The apostle is the first shepherd and he appoints subordinate shepherds as elders or overseers over the local churches. The original 12 Apostles were sent out by the Holy Spirit to aid the helpless and harassed of the flock. The Lord Jesus shepherds, or rules, through His apostles and elders. This authority is not given to these shepherds to dominate the flock with harshness or brutality. The good shepherd does not serve money, but the Lord. Good shepherds are appointed to take care of the flock. The godly shepherd is to strengthen the weak, heal the sick, bind up the injured, bring back strays, and search for the lost. The heart of each good shepherd is willing to lay down his own life for the sheep like the Good Shepherd, Jesus did.

Book Two

Apostles and Kings

Chapter 5

The Theme of Anointing

Over 600 References

The theme of anointing is one of the most important in the Bible. The New International Bible has 141 direct references to *anoint* in its various forms—*anoint, anointed, anointing,* and *anointed one.* The importance of these references is magnified by understanding that the New Testament writers also used a Greek word, transliterated into *Christ,* which means literally "the Anointed One," to refer to Jesus. *Christ* and *Messiah* were transliterated from Greek and Hebrew, respectively.

The New Testament makes 530 references to this all-important word *Christ.* There are also two references to the word *Messiah* in the New Testament. These have the same meaning. These references are found in John 1:41 and John 4:25. Simple math produces a total of over 670 references in the Scriptures to the word *anoint* in some form, with the majority of these references occurring in the New Testament. It is not too difficult to see that this is an important theme in the Scriptures and worthy of our attention in general. It is also specifically important to our examination of apostles.

Three Kinds of Anointed Ones

Occasionally in the Old Testament God anointed a particular person with ability and wisdom to perform an unusual and normally one-time task, such as building the temple or creating special objects for the tabernacle. However, from generation after generation God chose individuals and families that were anointed to perform three specific ongoing ministries among God's people, the Israelites.

It is from these three kinds of anointed ones—priests, prophets, and kings—that we derived our basic understanding of who and what the Anointed One, the Christ, would be. The New Testament writers started with this basic understanding that the Christ would be the fulfillment of the combination of all three of these anointed ones. Historically, several individuals had combined two of these roles, such as Melchisedek who was a priest and a king, David who was a king and a prophet, and Ezekiel who was a priest and a prophet. We might include Samuel, Deborah, and Moses as fulfilling dual roles as well. Samuel was a prophet and the last judge. Deborah was a prophetess and a judge. Moses was of the tribe of Levi and therefore could be considered a priest. He was also certainly a dynamic prophet.

One of the primary messages of the Gospel writers was the presentation of Jesus as the long-awaited Christ. The New Testament writers clearly desired to reveal the Lord Jesus in the three-fold fulfillment of these roles as Prophet, Priest, and King. The Book of Hebrews, for example, gives us a clear presentation and explanation of Jesus as our High Priest and King according to the order of Melchisedek.

The First References to *Anoint*

It is interesting that the first reference to *anoint* in the Old Testament refers to Abraham. Other renowned men of God lived before Abraham, yet this is the first reference that serves to point us to the Anointed One. This is not an accident. The Abrahamic covenant and the New Covenant are intimately related, as Paul shows us in the New Testament. Christ came to us as a fulfillment of the Abrahamic covenant.

These first references to anointing in the Old Testament begin to help us define what is meant by *anoint* and *anointing*. In the following Scripture God reminds Abraham of his anointing of a pillar as an act of consecration.

*I am the God of Bethel, where you **anointed** a pillar and where you made a vow to Me* (Genesis 31:13a).

The Special Anointing Oil

This and other references clearly state that Abraham anointed this pillar with oil, probably olive oil. The Old Testament lists many other references to the anointing of objects for use in worship. However, after the Exodus of the children of Israel from Egypt, these objects of worship were anointed with a special compound of oil and spices that created a sacred anointing oil, rather than with simple olive oil.

*Make these into a sacred **anointing** oil, a fragrant blend, the work of a perfumer. It will be the sacred **anointing** oil* (Exodus 30:25).

Some examples of the use of this sacred anointing oil are found in Exodus 29:36; Leviticus 8:11; and Numbers 7:10,84,88. In these references the altar of sacrifice and its utensils are anointed with this special oil. The anointing of the tent of meeting (the tabernacle) is found in Exodus 30:26, 40:9; Leviticus 8:10; and Numbers 7:1. Many other examples in the Old Testament also point toward the Anointed One, Christ.

Anointed Priests

Moses was to first anoint the tent of meeting and then to anoint Aaron and his sons as the first priests with this sacred anointing oil, consecrating them for service.

*After you put these clothes on your brother Aaron and his sons, **anoint** and ordain them. Consecrate them so they may serve Me as priests* (Exodus 28:41).

The Lord elaborates on this priesthood later when He says:

*Anoint them just as you **anointed** their father, so they may serve Me as priests. Their **anointing** will be to a priesthood that will continue for all generations to come* (Exodus 40:15).

From this point on in the Old Testament, the priest is periodically referred to as the anointed priest. (Some of the other references to the anointed priest are found in Leviticus 4:5,16, 6:22; Numbers 3:3.)

> *If the **anointed** priest sins, bringing guilt on the people, he must bring to the Lord a young bull without defect as a sin offering for the sin he has committed* (Leviticus 4:3).

Anointed Kings

After the period of the judges, God spoke to Samuel about anointing Israel's first king, Saul:

> *About this time tomorrow I will send you a man from the land of Benjamin. **Anoint** him leader over My people Israel; he will deliver My people from the hand of the Philistines. I have looked upon My people, for their cry has reached Me* (1 Samuel 9:16).

The next day Samuel obeyed the Lord and anointed Saul as king over Israel.

> *Then Samuel took a flask of oil and poured it on Saul's head and kissed him, saying, "Has not the Lord **anointed** you leader over His inheritance?"* (1 Samuel 10:1)

There will be more to say in a specific sense about this and other kings as types of apostles later in this work. Throughout the Old Testament there are numerous references to kings as being anointed. There are also a large number of references to *prince*. Translators in all versions I am aware of have been inconsistent in this translation. The New International Version has a mixture of differing Hebrew words all translated *prince* as well. The problem may be that Hebrew has many more differing words relating to royalty than English. Therefore, kings are clearly the group most frequently related to the word anointed, while the third group of anointed persons in the Old Testament, the prophets, have the fewest references.

Anointed Prophets

One reference in the Old Testament gives the command to Elijah the prophet to anoint both a king and a prophet. God speaks to Elijah these words:

*Also, **anoint** Jehu son of Nimshi **king** over Israel, and **anoint** Elisha son of Shaphat from Abel Meholah **to succeed you as prophet** (1 Kings 19:16).*

Old Testament Ministries Are Fulfilled in Jesus the Christ

It is no longer a mystery that Jesus is the fulfillment of this threefold ministry of the Old Testament. Hundreds of references to the Christ in the New Testament are no mystery. However, the New Testament writers mention it in other ways. From the following reference, it is evident that God Himself anointed Jesus without man's involvement.

*Indeed Herod and Pontius Pilate met together with the Gentiles and the people of Israel in this city to conspire against Your holy servant Jesus, **whom You anointed** (Acts 4:27).*

Another reference shows us that Jesus was not anointed with oil like the Old Testament priests, prophets, and kings, but He was anointed with the Holy Spirit and power.

*How **God anointed Jesus of Nazareth with the Holy Spirit and power**, and how He went around doing good and healing all who were under the power of the devil, because God was with Him (Acts 10:38).*

It should not be overlooked that the writer of the Book of Hebrews spends many verses explaining how Jesus is the new High Priest of an order different than that of the Old Testament Levitical order. There are also many verses dedicated to showing that Jesus is the Prophet and King. There is little debate among those who call on the name of the Lord and honor the Scriptures that Jesus is the fulfillment of these prophetic passages and that faith in Him enables Him to perform these roles on our behalf. However, merely understanding that He fulfills these roles is not enough for the purposes of this study. We must also understand the particular functions of each of these "types": the Old Testament priest, prophet, and king.

All Believers: New Testament Anointed Ones

The New Testament writers had a desire to illustrate the transitory nature of the ministry of the Old Testament as it pointed to the new ministry God was establishing through His Son. The most important change to the Old Testament threefold ministry as it passed into fulfillment in Christ and was reestablished as the New Covenant ministry is that *all* God's New Testament people are anointed by the Spirit. Each has a place of service and function in His Body, the Church.

John refers to this anointing in his letters. It seems that we could substitute "the presence of the Holy Spirit" in each place where the term *anointing* appears and not substantially change the meaning. However, the use of the term *anointing* intimately connects us as believers with the Anointed One, the Lord Jesus Christ. We each receive the same anointing of the Holy Spirit that He had during His earthly ministry and presently has in His heavenly ministry of intercession.

> *But you have an **anointing** from the Holy One, and all of you know the truth* (1 John 2:20).

Just a few verses later, John tells us again of the anointing we have received from Christ:

> *As for you, the **anointing** you received from Him remains in you, and you do not need anyone to teach you. But as His **anointing** teaches you about all things and as that **anointing** is real, not counterfeit—just as it has taught you, remain in Him* (1 John 2:27).

From these passages it is evident that being called "Christians" has more meaning than simply being followers of Jesus Christ. We are now the *anointed* of the Lord. We are anointed by the Spirit of God. The "anointing" of the Old Testament ministry has been fulfilled in Christ and transferred to those who are in Him.

New Testament Priests, Prophets, and Kings

Peter reveals in his letters that the functions of the Old Testament priesthood have been transferred to the entire Church. Peter also tells us that this is a "royal" priesthood. This reveals that the functions of the anointed king and priest have their fulfillment in the Church, which includes every believer.

*But you are a chosen people, **a royal priesthood**, a holy nation, a people belonging to God, that you may declare the praises of Him who called you out of darkness into His wonderful light* (1 Peter 2:9).

This is not entirely a New Testament doctrine, however. We find the same desire expressed by the Lord about His people, Israel.

*"You will be for Me **a kingdom of priests** and a holy nation." These are the words you are to speak to the Israelites* (Exodus 19:6).

Although all His people were to be priests and holy to Him, God still designated a particular family of the tribe of Levi to perform the actual specific function of priesthood. Some have suggested that God was disappointed in Israel for not becoming a nation of priests and therefore appointed one particular tribe. I find nothing in the Bible to substantiate this belief and believe it to be simple conjecture. All of Israel were to be priests, and yet one tribe was designated to perform this function.

In a similar fashion, all believers are anointed ones and are called to minister to God. All the functions of the Old Testament anointed ones are transferred to the Body of Christ. However, some are called to roles strongly similar to those of Old Testament anointed ones.

The Old Testament prophet likewise is revealed in the Body of Christ in that every believer can exercise the gift of prophecy and receive revelational gifts from God to edify the Body of Christ. This transformation was prophesied by Joel and repeated by Peter on the day of Pentecost when God began to anoint His New Covenant servants with the Holy Spirit:

> *No, this is what was spoken by the prophet Joel: "In the last days, God says, I will pour out My Spirit on all people. **Your sons and daughters will prophesy**, your **young men will see visions, your old men will dream dreams**. Even on My servants, both men and women, I will pour out My Spirit in those days, and they will **prophesy**"* (Acts 2:16-18).

All born-again believers, all who are baptized in His Spirit, are anointed and are able to function at some level in the roles of priest, prophet, and king. In fact, one of the New Testament's most important revelations is that each believer has a specific, important, and essential function in the Body of Christ.

A Problem of Balance

Each believer has an important ministry calling in the Body of Christ. This is wonderful and undeniable. However, this does not mean that God has not reestablished these three specific functions of Old Testament ministry within the New Testament fivefold ministry. It is a delicate problem of balance. Acknowledging the reestablishment of the threefold Old Testament ministry in the fivefold ministry of the New Testament cannot validate the error of separating the Body of Christ into clergy and laity. All God's people are anointed as His servants, but some have callings that closely parallel the Old Testament ministries. This is also wonderful and undeniable. We must acknowledge that these ministries exist in the Church era. Not to acknowledge this is to err again in reaction to former heresies. The truth has a balance. All God's people are anointed for service to Him. There are some, however, who have ministries that parallel and take their pattern from Old Testament ministries.

Transfer of Old Testament Ministry Functions

The chart below illustrates in a small degree what has happened to the Old Testament ministry functions. They have been fulfilled in Christ.

Old Testament				New Testament
Priest	⇒fulfilled by	⇒Christ	⇒revealed by	⇒Pastor/Teacher
Prophet	⇒fulfilled by	⇒Christ	⇒revealed by	⇒Prophet
King	⇒fulfilled by	⇒Christ	⇒revealed by	⇒Apostle

It is apparent that Jesus, the Anointed One, was and is the fulfillment of all of the various ministries given to the Church. Jesus the Christ is revealed through His various ministries. He is the Apostle. He is the Prophet. He is the Evangelist. He is the Shepherd. He is the Teacher. He is also the fruit of the Spirit; love, joy, peace, patience; the rest are simply the character of Jesus Christ being made manifest to distribute and reveal His Son in the Body of Christ in wonderful ways. The nine gifts of the Holy Spirit are also expressions of the ministry of Jesus Christ. Jesus is revealed in His power, grace, knowledge, wisdom, and compassion in the gifts of the Holy Spirit. In other words, God has distributed and revealed His Son in the Body of Christ in wonderful ways. Each of these New Covenant ministries has an anointing. That is, each ministry has a particular presence and function of Jesus, the Anointed One, through the work of the Holy Spirit.

Among Pentecostals and Charismatics, these five ministries have been called the fivefold ministry. Some, however, believe that there are really only four ministries. They have suggested that the ministry of the pastor always includes the teacher and that the Greek construction of Ephesians 4:11 recommends this belief. Yet after study of other passages, such as First Corinthians 12, where the teacher is listed and the pastor is not, it is hard not to support the fivefold-ministry view that the teaching ministry can stand alone without being included in the pastoral ministry. However, it is exceedingly clear that the pastoral ministry must also teach in order to fulfill its function. This will be abundantly revealed as the study of these ministries continues, focusing on understanding the Old Testament threefold ministry as types of the New Testament ministry.

Old Testament Types of New Testament Ministries

These Old Testament anointed ones are types of some of the New Testament ministries as well as types of Christ. The New Testament writers were more than just acquainted with this Old Testament understanding of the threefold anointed ones. To be sure, it was paramount in their understanding, as the Old Testament was the only Bible of the early Church for a significant period of time until the various gospels and letters were copied, circulated, collected, and later accepted as canon.

The term *canon* literally means "the rule." The 39 books of the Old Testament were considered canon and were little disputed by the time Jesus the Christ was born. The 27 books of the New Testament, however, were not canonized until several centuries after the time of the early Church. While it is not the purpose of this work to recount the history of the formation of the New Testament canon, it is important to acknowledge that the New Testament did not simply fall out of Heaven in its present form. It was still being written as the first apostles walked the earth. The Old Testament, however, in its Greek form, the Septuagint, was in its final canonized form. It was widely circulated and used by the Gentile and Hellenistic Jewish early Church while the documents of the New Testament were still being written, circulated, copied, and collected. To be sure, the Old Testament ministries were clearly in the minds of those who were writing the New Testament.

The Ministry of the Evangelist

The ministry of the evangelist, as well as many other ministries noted in the New Testament, was not included in the earlier chart.

The evangelist and other ministries, such as those listed in First Corinthians 12:28, are unique to the Church age and not clearly patterned, or typed, by the Old Testament anointed ones. The evangelist in particular is a ministry focused upon the "lost" rather than upon God's people. It is a testimony to the grace of God being offered to all.

This in no way reduces the importance of the ministry of the evangelist to the Church and the world at large. Although this ministry has no clear relationship to the anointed ones of the Old Testament, it has an obvious connection to the ministry of those pure spirit beings referred to as angels in both the Old and New Testaments. The word *evangelist* is transliterated from the Greek word *euangelistes*. This is a compound word in Greek. The *eu* means in English "well or good." The Greek word *angelos* is the word from which we transliterate "angel." The word *angelos* also has been properly translated "messenger" in various passages. Putting the two Greek words together, it means "messenger of good."

The ministry of angels as messengers of God in the Old and New Testaments brings to mind the function of the herald in the Old Testament. A herald was a messenger sent with a particular message to deliver. Normally heralds were in the employ of a king. The evangelist is a herald of King Jesus Christ, taking the message of the Kingdom of God to those who haven't heard.

Until the revealing of the Messiah in the first century, there was no distinct message to proclaim to the world. Indeed, the Covenant-making God of Israel had primarily confined the revelation of Himself to the descendants of Abraham and a few important persons outside Israel. However, the New Testament strongly reveals the desire of God to be revealed and glorified among the nations. The ministry of the evangelist is intimately connected to this presently revealed desire and will of God to bless the nations.

Ministry Functions in Common

Before exploring the transfer of these specific ministries' functions into New Testament ministry, it is necessary to state what all fivefold ministries have in common. All five ministries preach and teach the Word of God. All ministries work to prepare God's people for service to Him. All ministries will edify (build up) the Church. All of these ministries have functions that are in common and should be motivated for the same purpose outlined in Ephesians 4.

It was He who gave some to be apostles, some to be prophets, some to be evangelists, and some to be pastors and teachers, to prepare God's people for works of service, so that the body of Christ may be built up until we all reach unity in the faith and in the knowledge of the Son of God and become mature, attaining to the whole measure of the fullness of Christ (Ephesians 4:11-13).

These ministries are to function until a unity of the faith occurs. They are to function until the Church is filled with the knowledge of the Son of God. They are to function until the Church becomes mature. They are also to function until the Church attains to the whole measure of the fullness of Christ.

Summary of Chapter Five
The Old Testament threefold anointed ministry of priests, prophets, and kings is fulfilled in Jesus Christ, the Anointed One. The fivefold ministry of the New Testament is the expression of Jesus, the Anointed One, through the Church. Each of the ministry gifts is the revelation of Jesus, the Anointed One, by the Holy Spirit. All God's people are anointed ones fulfilling the Old Testament threefold ministry. The fivefold ministry, however, demonstrates these threefold Old Testament functions more specifically than the average believer. Therefore, these Old Testament ministries become types of New Testament ministries. The Old Testament priest becomes a type of the New Testament pastor. The Old Testament prophet becomes a type of the New Testament prophet. The Old Testament king becomes a type of the New Testament apostle.

Chapter 6

The Ministry Functions of the Priest and Prophet

Transfer of Ministry Functions

This chapter will consider the transfer of anointed ministry functions from the Old Testament priest to the New Testament pastor and from the Old Testament prophet to the New Testament prophet. After laying this important groundwork, we will consider the king as a type of the apostle.

As we have already stated, the threefold ministry of the Old Testament anointed ones—the priest, prophet, and king—have been fulfilled in Jesus Christ. We can now see Jesus the Priest revealed and expressed clearly in the ministry of the New Testament pastor. As stated before, every believer is a priest unto God, but the pastor expresses this function in a greater degree and in specific ways that the ordinary believer does not.

Concise Description of Old Testament Priest

A concise description of the ministry of the numerous Levitical priests can be found in Moses' words to the Levites in his blessing of the 12 tribes of Israel.

> *About Levi he said: "Your Thummim and Urim belong to the man You favored. You tested him at Massah; You*

contended with him at the waters of Meribah. He said of his father and mother, 'I have no regard for them.' He did not recognize his brothers or acknowledge his own children, but he watched over Your word and guarded Your covenant. He teaches Your precepts to Jacob and Your law to Israel. He offers incense before You and whole burnt offerings on Your altar. Bless all his skills, O Lord, and be pleased with the work of his hands. Smite the loins of those who rise up against him; strike his foes till they rise no more" (Deuteronomy 33:8-11).

From this passage we can discern quite a number of the responsibilities of the Old Testament priest. We will attempt to elaborate on them phrase by phrase as well as cite other passages of Scripture that detail and clarify these priestly functions.

Leadership of Worship

In the passage above, we see that the Old Testament priest had responsibilities for leading the people of God in worship. It tells us:

*He **offers** incense before You and whole burnt **offerings** on Your altar.*

The priest had the primary responsibility before God concerning the practice of worship. The priest was to maintain the daily sacrifices, offer incense, and perform other aspects of tabernacle (and later temple) worship. He was to administer the special annual sacrifices and ensure they were done properly. He interacted daily with the people of God who were seeking to please God through the Law.

This leadership of worship is clearly the ministry of the pastor in the Church age. The pastor is responsible for the day-to-day ministry of the local church in strikingly similar fashion to the Old Testament priest. He may delegate this work to others, but he alone is responsible for its quality and execution. He also plans and executes all the services during holiday periods, funerals, baptisms, and other events and special services for the local church. This is clearly equivalent to the function of the Old Testament priest.

Care of Worship Facilities and Articles

The priest had the responsibility of maintaining the place of meeting, the articles of worship, the altar, and so on. He also collected the tithe as his own support and offerings to maintain the meeting place and instruments of worship.

It could not be clearer that this function of the Old Testament priest is now the domain of the local pastor. He is responsible for the upkeep of his church's property. He should also be the recipient of the tithe for his own support. Offerings should also be used for the maintenance and purchase of physical property to be able to conduct ministry in the best fashion possible. These are rather obvious and similar characteristics of both the Levitical priest and the New Testament pastor.

Responsibility in Teaching

While this function is not obvious to most believers today, one of the primary tasks of the Levitical priest was to teach the Law of God to the people of God. Deuteronomy 33:10 shows us that the priest taught the precepts and law of God.

*He **teaches** Your precepts to Jacob and Your law to Israel.*

The priest gave instruction to all, young priests, prophets, and kings included. This verse out of Second Chronicles also reveals this ministry function:

*For a long time Israel was without the true God, without a **priest to teach** and without the law* (2 Chronicles 15:3).

This teaching function of the priest, now primarily in the domain of the pastor, is revealed in several passages. The terms *overseer, elder,* and *pastor* are equivalent terms in the New Testament, which is clarified in an appendix of this work. The overseer must be able to teach to fulfill his God-given duties.

*Now the **overseer** must be above reproach, the husband of
but one wife, temperate, self-controlled, respectable, hospitable, **able to teach** (1 Timothy 3:2).*

Likewise, the Scripture tells us that the pastoral elder who
works hard at teaching is worthy of double honor:

*The **elders** who direct the affairs of the church well are
worthy of double honor, especially those whose work is
preaching and **teaching** (1 Timothy 5:17).*

Additionally, the elder who is also an overseer must be able to
encourage others with sound doctrine. Paul in this passage uses the
terms *elder* and *overseer* interchangeably. It is clear that these are
two words for the same ministry, one describing the function
(overseer) and the other describing the office (elder).

*An **elder** must be blameless, the husband of but one wife, a
man whose children believe and are not open to the charge
of being wild and disobedient. Since an **overseer** is entrusted with God's work, he must be blameless—not overbearing, not quick-tempered, not given to drunkenness, not
violent, not pursuing dishonest gain. Rather he must be hospitable, one who loves what is good, who is self-controlled,
upright, holy and disciplined. **He must hold firmly to the
trustworthy message** as it has been taught, so that he can
encourage others by **sound doctrine** and refute those who
oppose it (Titus 1:6-9).*

Counseling and Guidance

From our opening passage in Deuteronomy 33, we find this
statement about the priest that focuses our attention on his ability
to discern the will of God and make decisions:

Your Thummim and Urim belong to the man You favored.

Priests were to provide guidance and pronounce verdicts. Normally, the priest ministered to the common people but could minister to important people. The High Priest maintained the Urim

and Thummim, which apparently were used to discern the will of God in certain matters. How the Urim and Thummim were precisely used is not evident from the Scriptures. Since the Holy Spirit and the canon of the Scripture have been given to guide us in this age, speculation on this Old Testament phenomena seems pointless beyond indicating that the priest had a special means, probably casting lots, to indicate the will of God. Those who want to take this further may find themselves on the edge of cultism, or worse, occultism.

It seems that the Urim and Thummim were devices used in casting lots. These particular words in Hebrew appear to be derived from words that could be taken to mean *positive* and *negative*.[1] Fortunately (or unfortunately), the Scriptures give us little practical information about the Urim and Thummim. The following passage describes this particular function of judging matters. This passage speaks again to the teaching ministry of the priesthood as well.

> *Go to the priests, who are Levites, and to the judge who is in office at that time. Inquire of them and **they will give you the verdict**. You must act according to the **decisions** they give you at the place the Lord will choose. Be careful to do everything they direct you to do. Act according to the law they **teach** you and the **decisions** they give you. Do not turn aside from what they tell you, to the right or to the left. The man who shows contempt for the judge or for the priest who stands ministering there to the Lord your God must be put to death. You must purge the evil from Israel. All the people will hear and be afraid, and will not be contemptuous again* (Deuteronomy 17:9-13).

Anyone who is acquainted with the ministry of the present-day pastor should be able to see that this is clearly within his function. No one else in the Church offers as much to God's people in the

---

1.   pg. 228, *The New Bible Commentary: Revised.*

area of counseling and guidance. Pastors are also often called upon to settle minor disputes among God's people. Any believer who does not listen to his pastor in regard to matters involving other members of the congregation is certainly in need of basic training in discipleship. Any believer who does not seek out his pastor and reveal his struggle when there are serious disputes within his own family needs further training in humility and wisdom.

Examples of Holiness Before the People

God expected the priest to serve Him faithfully. He could not put even the perceived interests of his family before his ministry. The passage we began with, Deuteronomy 33, defines this ministry for us. It relates that the Levites had historically made a commitment to God to serve Him above their own families. This refers to the events found in Exodus 32:25-29. In this situation, the Levites took up swords against their own rebellious relatives in obedience to God's command through Moses. This passage says:

> *"He said of his father and mother, 'I have no regard for them.' He did not recognize his brothers or acknowledge his own children, but he watched over Your word and guarded Your covenant"* (Deuteronomy 33:9).

These men were to regard their ministries as more important than their families, and they were to maintain personal holiness and integrity in their conduct in ministry. Jesus Himself told us that we could not love our spouses, our parents, or our children more than Him. Every servant of God will face times when he must choose the will of God over the desires of his family. The servant of God cannot be bound by the fear of man, family or otherwise.

Balancing this truth is a corresponding truth that every servant of God must also see his family as a God-given priority in his service to God. To neglect his family is to neglect the first ministry that God has given him. The Holy Spirit must guide us in how to properly apply these conflicting thoughts in each situation that may arise.

The priest was to be an outstanding example of holiness before the people of God. This is not to say that prophets and kings could live unrighteously, but because the priest was continually before the people doing his ministry, he became their primary example of what a man of God should be. Additionally, the following passage reveals that the personal conduct of the priest mattered to God. We see once again in this passage that the priestly ministry of teaching is confirmed.

> *Then the Lord said to Aaron, "You and your sons are **not to drink wine or other fermented drink whenever you go into the Tent of Meeting**, or you will die. This is a lasting ordinance for the generations to come. **You must distinguish between the holy and the common, between the unclean and the clean**, and you must **teach** the Israelites all the decrees the Lord has given them through Moses"* (Leviticus 10:8-11).

The New Testament pastor is likewise expected to set an example for the people of God. His teaching ministry will mean little if he somehow thinks that his example is unimportant. More will be taught by his flock's observation of his day-to-day life than a lifetime of verbal teaching. The same passages that describe the teaching ministry of the pastor also speak to the lifestyle of the godly pastor.

> *Now the **overseer** must be above reproach, the husband of but one wife, temperate, self-controlled, respectable, hospitable, able to teach* (1 Timothy 3:2).

The pastor must be above reproach and blameless, with excellent character and behavior. He must have a stable marriage and family life. His example before the Church is made of obvious importance in this passage. His teaching ministry will only be effective if he maintains an excellent reputation.

> *An **elder** must be blameless, the husband of but one wife, a man whose children believe and are not open to the charge*

*of being wild and disobedient. Since an **overseer** is entrusted with God's work, he must be blameless—not overbearing, not quick-tempered, not given to drunkenness, not violent, not pursuing dishonest gain. Rather he must be hospitable, one who loves what is good, who is self-controlled, upright, holy and disciplined. He must hold firmly to the trustworthy message as it has been taught, so that he can **encourage others by sound doctrine and refute those who oppose it*** (Titus 1:6-9).

Hopefully by now the reader can see the relationship between the pastor and the priest. Clearly there is much more to say to describe either ministry completely, but that has not been the object of this portion of this work. It is enough to say at present that the priestly ministry has been fulfilled in the High Priestly ministry of Jesus as related in the Book of Hebrews. This ministry is then transformed into and revealed by the New Testament ministry of the pastor. We will now turn our attention to the second anointed one, the Old Testament prophet.

The Ministry of the Prophet

It is necessary to establish some understanding of the relationship of the Old Testament anointed ones of priests, prophets, and kings to the New Testament ministry in order to have more clarity about the ministry of the apostle. So our attention will be upon the transformation of the fulfilled Old Testament prophet into the ministry of the New Testament prophet. In review, we remind the reader that the Old Testament prophet was fulfilled in Christ, the Prophet, and now the ministry of the New Testament prophet is revealing Christ as Prophet once again.

As we have already noted, the prophet was one of God's anointed ones in the Old Testament. When the New Testament speaks of prophets, it does not explain or elaborate on this ministry as it does the ministry of the apostle. The reason is fairly easy to discern. No one familiar with the history of Israel would have been unfamiliar with the role of the prophet.

The general lack of explanation of the New Testament prophet in Scripture testifies that the role is basically unchanged from the Old Testament prophet, despite what the doctrines of men may say. Among Evangelical Christians of all types are doctrines that either deny the reality of this ministry in the Church today or discredit it by suggesting it is unreliable or that it is somehow less than the ministry of the Old Testament prophet. We must not reduce what God has exalted as second. To suggest that the New Testament prophetic ministry is less than that of the Old Testament contradicts God's Word in several places—directly and indirectly. (See Matthew 11:11; Second Corinthians 3:6-11.) A careful study of the ministry of the Old Testament prophet provides insight into the role of the New Testament prophet.

The New Testament Prophet

There are many within the Church who have not understood that there is a New Testament expression of this Old Testament ministry. The Old Testament ministry is clearly revealed, as explained previously, and therefore the New Testament does very little to expound this ministry to us as we would otherwise expect. However, the Christian prophet is revealed in passages like those found in the Book of Acts. For example, prophets associated with the church at Jerusalem visited and ministered at the church at Antioch.

*During this time some **prophets** came down from Jerusalem to Antioch* (Acts 11:27).

This was the time that Paul and Barnabas were in Antioch. The passage tells us that one of these prophets, Agabus, predicted a famine that took place during the reign of Caesar Claudius. It is certain that Paul and Barnabas knew Agabus personally. We will relate more about Agabus later. These prophets were not the only ones known to the church at Antioch. In Acts 13, a possible listing of the elders of the church of Antioch, we learn that there were also prophets there. Because of the way this verse is constructed, it is impossible to say which persons were prophets and which were

teachers. There must have been at least two of each if we are going
to take the plural forms of each word seriously.

*In the church at Antioch there were **prophets** and teachers:
Barnabas, Simeon called Niger, Lucius of Cyrene, Manaen
(who had been brought up with Herod the tetrarch) and
Saul* (Acts 13:1).

We also learn of two more prophets, Judas and Silas, who were
involved in ministry along with Paul and Barnabas. These men
were sent with Paul and Barnabas as representatives of the apostles and elders at Jerusalem to be witnesses of the decision of this
Council addressing the controversy over the relationship of the
Law of Moses and the Gentile believers. Again, Paul is interacting
with those who have prophetic calls on their lives.

*Judas and Silas, who themselves were **prophets**, said much
to encourage and strengthen the brothers* (Acts 15:32).

If we assume there were at least two prophets present in each
of the passages above where the plural is used, then we can count
a minimum of six prophets from these passages alone. However,
we must acknowledge that there must have been many more from
the following passages found in Paul's writings. From the testimony of Scripture we can determine that the ministry of the Christian prophet was not rare for the early Church, and that it was
considered as second only to the apostolic ministry.

*And **in the church** God has appointed first of all apostles,
second prophets, third teachers, then workers of miracles,
also those having gifts of healing, those able to help others,
those with gifts of administration, and those speaking in
different kinds of tongues. Are all apostles? Are all **prophets**? Are all teachers? Do all work miracles?* (1 Corinthians 12:28-29)

Paul also lists this ministry gift as second to apostles in the
Book of Ephesians:

*It was He who gave some to be apostles, some to be **prophets**, some to be evangelists, and some to be pastors and teachers* (Ephesians 4:11).

Paul indicates that he expected there would be more than one prophet in any gathering of God's people. In this case, two or three prophets were to speak and other prophets were to judge what was spoken. If we do some math from this passage, adding the prophets speaking ("two or three") to the "others" judging (meaning at least two), we find the sum to be at least four or five prophets in each local church.

*Two or three **prophets** should speak, and the **others** should weigh carefully what is said* (1 Corinthians 14:29; see also 14:32,37).

Paul in these passages also tells us that the Christian prophet is second to the apostle. The indication of "second" does not reveal the relationship between these first and second ministries; however, the Word of God is not silent concerning this relationship. In Ephesians Paul places these ministries together as the foundation of the Church. There is no question that he is referring to the Christian prophet rather than the Old Testament prophet because he says that both apostle and prophet are the foundation with Christ Jesus as Cornerstone.

If Paul were referring to the Old Testament prophet rather than the New Testament prophet, then he could not tell us that Jesus Christ was the cornerstone of this foundation. The Church is built upon the foundation of Christ. The Old Testament prophet is not part of the Church and therefore is not built upon the cornerstone of Christ.

[God's household is] *built on the foundation of the apostles and **prophets**, with Christ Jesus Himself as the chief cornerstone* (Ephesians 2:20).

Paul places these ministries together again as those that are revelational by the Holy Spirit. Paul tells us that God is now revealing His mysteries to prophets, clearly indicating that he is speaking about Christian prophets.

> *...the mystery of Christ, which was not made known to men in other generations as it has **now been revealed by the Spirit to God's** holy apostles and **prophets*** (Ephesians 3:4-5).

Trusting that these passages are enough to establish that the New Testament reveals the Christian prophet to be an expected and welcomed function of the Spirit of Jesus Christ, we will now review what the Old Testament reveals about the actual functions of this important ministry.

Functions of the Prophet

Contrary to popular belief, there were generally many prophets living in Israel at the same time. Of course, there were always considerably fewer than the thousands of priests. Not all of God's prophets were reliable or faithful to God, despite their calling. For the most part, the Old Testament concentrates on the faithful prophets of the Lord, but it does not neglect to tell us of those who were less than pleasing to God. In passages where God speaks correction to His prophets, there is much to be learned about the prophetic role. We will look at some of these corrections. The following are the ministry functions of the prophet.

The Ministry of Revelation

Probably the most essential ministry function of the prophet is to *stand in the council of the Lord.* This is a ministry of revelation that hears and sees what the Lord is saying for a particular situation, nation, city, person, or persons. All other prophetic ministry functions are related to and flow from this one. This is the characteristic that makes a prophet a prophet.

> *But which of them has **stood in the council of the Lord** to see or to hear His word? Who has listened and heard His word? See, the storm of the Lord will burst out in wrath, a whirlwind swirling down on the heads of the wicked. The*

anger of the Lord will not turn back until He fully accomplishes the purposes of His heart. In days to come you will understand it clearly. I did not send these prophets, yet they have run with their message; I did not speak to them, yet they have prophesied. But if they had stood in My council, they would have proclaimed My words to My people and would have turned them from their evil ways and from their evil deeds (Jeremiah 23:18-22).

This is clearly correction from God to those who are prophets, but were not sent by God with a message. However, within this passage we learn much about the role of the true prophet. He *stands in the council of the Lord* and *proclaims God's word to His people.* In saying this, there are those who would confuse the issue by improperly substituting *preaching* for *prophecy.*

Prophecy Is Not Preaching

There are some who have mistranslated and misunderstood this as referring to the preaching ministry. Most mature prophets are also preachers, but not all modern Christian prophets preach. Some may only function in the ministry of revelation and prophecy. Not all preachers are prophets, nor do they all stand in the council of the Lord as a regular part of their ministry. Preaching is not necessarily prophetic. It can instruct, encourage, and exhort without ever moving into a prophetic flow and gifting. The prophet will bring to the circumstance the specific word of God for the moment, for the individual, for the local church. This is what sets him apart from the ordinary preacher of God's word.

Prophetic Revelation from Dreams and Visions

This prophetic revelation can come in the form of a vision or dream. Although God may speak to all His servants through dreams and visions from time to time, this is an ongoing experience with the prophet.

He said, "Listen to My words: 'When a prophet of the Lord is among you, I reveal Myself to him in visions, I speak to him in dreams' " (Numbers 12:6).

Revelation also may come often to the prophet in the form of words. The prophet Gad regularly ministered to David in this manner. Apparently during the night or early morning, God would speak His word into the prophet's spirit for him to deliver to King David in the morning.

Before David got up the next morning, the word of the Lord had come to Gad the prophet, David's seer (2 Samuel 24:11).

Other passages show this revelational ministry of the prophet. In Second Kings chapter 3, three kings found themselves in a difficult situation and sought out the prophet Elisha for guidance.

But Jehoshaphat asked, "Is there no prophet of the Lord here, that we may inquire of the Lord through him?" An officer of the king of Israel answered, "Elisha son of Shaphat is here. He used to pour water on the hands of Elijah." Jehoshaphat said, "The word of the Lord is with him." So the king of Israel and Jehoshaphat and the king of Edom went down to him. ... Elisha said, "As surely as the Lord Almighty lives, whom I serve, if I did not have respect for the presence of Jehoshaphat king of Judah, I would not look at you or even notice you" (2 Kings 3:11-12,14).

This passage illustrates that the ministry of the prophet is primarily revelational. The three kings believed they would determine the particular will of God for their situation by consulting with the prophet Elisha. They knew the word of God was with him in a revelational sense. Elisha also gives us a description of himself in the passage in the last verse. "Whom I serve" states his relationship with God. Modern translation has obscured this passage, as well as many others. The New American Standard version translates this phrase as "before whom I stand," which reiterates the relationship of the prophet to God. The prophet stands in the council of the Lord.

God spoke to the prophet Jeremiah about his role as a prophet. Unfortunately, the meaning of this passage is also a somewhat obscured translation of the New International Version. It says this:

> *Therefore this is what the Lord says: "If you repent, I will restore you **that you may serve Me**; if you **utter worthy, not worthless, words,** you will be My spokesman. Let this people turn to you, but you must not turn to them. I will make you a wall to this people, a fortified wall of bronze; they will fight against you but will not overcome you, for I am with you to rescue and save you," declares the Lord* (Jeremiah 15:19-20).

The phrase *that you may serve Me* is translated, "before Me you will stand" in the New American Standard Version, which tries to approximate the most literal translation. Again, the ministry of the prophet is to stand in the council of the Lord and to utter worthy words of revelation by the Spirit.

It is possible, of course, that a person appearing to be a prophet could mislead God's people. The passage below speaks to that problem. This is one of those passages that is instructive through the corrections that God speaks; the Lord tells us what a proper prophet should be doing in the context of His correction. The proper prophet must speak visions from the mouth of the Lord and not from his own mind.

> *This is what the Lord Almighty says: "Do not listen to what the prophets are prophesying to you; they fill you with false hopes. They speak visions from their own minds, not **from the mouth of the Lord**"* (Jeremiah 23:16).

It is clear that dreams and visions come from the mouth of the Lord; however, His revealed word is a higher form of revelation and is compared with dreams as grain is compared with straw. In other words, grain is of more value. Lest we think that God is condemning all prophetic utterance, visions, and dreams, a few verses later the Lord encourages those who are prophets to faithfully speak the revelational word that comes from God.

*"Let the prophet who has a dream tell his dream, but **let the one who has My word speak it faithfully**. For what has straw to do with grain?" declares the Lord* (Jeremiah 23:28).

Prophets can also proclaim a message that the Lord has spoken and expect fulfillment of that word. Messages that predict events in a certain time or season that go unfulfilled by God become a way to measure the prophetic utterance and the prophet. However, it may not always be that simple. There were some positive prophecies that did not seem to be conditional as they were stated in the Old Testament that God did not fulfill because of the sin of the persons involved. On the other hand, there were some prophecies that were negative that God did not fulfill or delayed because of the humility and repentance of the persons involved. So the issue of fulfilled prophecy is not quite so simple, but it still remains a way to test the prophet. Nevertheless, Moses tells us to measure the prophet by measuring the fulfillment of his prophecies.

If what a prophet proclaims in the name of the Lord does not take place or come true, that is a message the Lord has not spoken. That prophet has spoken presumptuously. Do not be afraid of him (Deuteronomy 18:22).

Prophets Reveal Other Ministries

Prophets also have a function of revealing and anointing other ministries and calling them to their ministry functions, often revealing much of their future ministry. Our earlier discussion on the anointing has already shown much of this function.

*Jehu got up and went into the house. Then the **prophet** poured the oil on Jehu's head and declared, **"This is what the Lord, the God of Israel, says: 'I anoint you king over the Lord's people Israel**. You are to destroy the house of Ahab your master, and I will avenge the blood of My servants the prophets and the blood of all the Lord's servants shed by Jezebel'"* (2 Kings 9:6-7).

Prophets Issue Guidance and Warnings From God

Prophets also can issue guidance and warnings to God's people and His other anointed servants, to wicked individuals, to cities, and to nations. Often the warning will encourage repentance and returning to the Lord.

> *The Lord **warned** Israel and Judah **through all His prophets and seers:** "Turn from your evil ways. Observe My commands and decrees, in accordance with the entire Law that I commanded your fathers to obey and that I delivered to you through My servants the prophets. ... until the Lord removed them from His presence, as He had **warned through all His servants the prophets**. So the people of Israel were taken from their homeland into exile in Assyria, and they are still there* (2 Kings 17:13,23).

Prophets often have a message of repentance, of returning to God. Sometimes they are successful in producing repentance, sometimes not.

> *Although the Lord **sent prophets to the people to bring them back to Him**, and though they testified against them, they would not listen* (2 Chronicles 24:19).

The New Testament Prophet Agabus

The prophet Agabus is the only Christian prophet described by the New Testament in any detail. The two references to him in the Book of Acts are ten chapters apart. This implies that he had an ongoing ministry within the first-century Church. We see the ministry of revelation working in him. He clearly stood in the council of the Lord.

> *During this time some **prophets** came down from Jerusalem to Antioch. One of them, named **Agabus**, stood up and through the Spirit predicted that a severe famine would spread over the entire Roman world. (This happened during the reign of Claudius.)* (Acts 11:27-28)

In the second passage, ten chapters later, Agabus offers a very specific prophetic word of warning to Paul about future difficulties. His prophecy revealing a portion of Paul's future was very accurate, as the rest of the Book of Acts records.

> *After we had been there a number of days, **a prophet named Agabus** came down from Judea. Coming over to us, he took Paul's belt, tied his own hands and feet with it and said, "The Holy Spirit says, 'In this way the Jews of Jerusalem will bind the owner of this belt and will hand him over to the Gentiles' "* (Acts 21:10-11).

Two Old Testament prophetic functions of revelation and warning are found in the New Testament prophet Agabus. It is logical to conclude that all the functions of the Old Testament prophet will be found in the New Testament prophet. There are more references in the New Testament to the New Testament prophet's ministry than there are to the pastor, evangelist, or teacher. Paul places it in secondary importance only to the apostle, yet a high degree of confusion and ignorance remains regarding this ministry in the modern Church. This must change quickly for the sake of the Kingdom of God.

Summary of Chapter Six

All believers share in the anointing of Jesus, the Anointed One. All anointed believers experience to some degree the work of Jesus, the Anointed One, through them as priests and prophets. However, the New Testament pastor specifically expresses the ministry functions of the Old Testament priest to a greater degree than the average believer. Likewise, the New Testament prophet expresses the ministry functions of the Old Testament prophet more specifically and in a greater degree than the average believer. Therefore, these Old Testament ministries serve as strong "types" to help us to better understand them in this age.

Chapter 7

Kings as Types of Apostles

The ministries of the Old Testament priest and prophet are fulfilled in the New Testament fivefold ministry through the ministries of the New Testament pastor and prophet. The anointed king of the Old Testament was fulfilled in Christ and transformed into the New Testament ministry of the apostle.

Proper Limitation in the Use of Types

Teaching by the use of Old Testament types can be dangerous if the "truth" being taught is not supported by the clear teaching of the rest of the New Testament. It is easy to teach a pet doctrine by the use of types. Hopefully by the end of this book the reader will see the clear connections between these Old Testament and New Testament ministries, keeping in mind that any teaching on apostles from the Old Testament kings requires clear support from the rest of the New Testament.

The King as a Type of the Apostle

There are parallels between the ministry of the godly king and the ministry of the apostle, just as there were parallels between the ministries of the Old Testament priest and the New Testament pastor or between the Old Testament prophet and the New Testament prophet. Properly understood, if we use the king as a type of the apostle, we can gain a new understanding of apostolic ministry that would have been apparent to the early Church.

For example, the words of the Lord Jesus concerning the 12 Apostles illustrate the connection between the king and the apostle. Jesus tells the Twelve that they will sit upon thrones and will do the kingly task of judging:

> *Jesus said to them, "I tell you the truth, at the renewal of all things, when the Son of Man sits on His glorious throne, you who have followed Me will also sit on twelve **thrones, judging** the twelve tribes of Israel* (Matthew 19:28; see also Luke 22:30).

Paul illustrates this truth in First Corinthians 4:6 when he explains that he is speaking "in a figure," or using types, concerning apostles—specifically regarding himself and Apollos. He uses several types in this description, including that of the king. This can be easily missed in this passage, since Paul is using a corrective tone with the Corinthian church. He has previously noted their puffed-up attitude and their tendency to carnally compare one ministry with another. In the context of this passage, Paul is essentially saying that since the apostles, who are "kings," do not have a proud and arrogant attitude, then they who are not "kings" have no right to exalt one ministry over another. In an almost sarcastic tone he tells the Corinthians they have arrogantly "reigned without us [the apostles]."

> *Already you have all you want! Already you have become rich! You have become **kings**—and that without us! How I wish that you really had become **kings** so that we might be **kings** with you! For it seems to me that God has put **us apostles** on display at the end of the procession, like men condemned to die in the arena. We have been made a spectacle to the whole universe, to angels as well as to men* (1 Corinthians 4:8-9).

There are several interesting pictures in this passage. The first comes from the word that is translated as the phrase "on display." It can also be translated as "to show forth"; "set forth"; or "to declare." The Greek word is *apodeiknumi*, which is used as a technical term for exhibiting gladiators in the Roman arena. This explains the phrase "last of all." It is referring to the grand finale in the arena. The best fighters were kept until last to put on the best show for the audience.

This could be a hidden reference to the importance of spiritual warfare in the ministry of the apostle. No doubt Paul was referring to the historical fact that the apostles were following a long line of priests, prophets, and kings on display before the world. It may not have been his intention to make the connection here with the fact that both priests and prophets were in the arena long before the kings of Israel, but that fact should not escape us. This also could be a hidden prophetic indication that God will again clearly establish the ministry of the apostle to the Church last of all—before the end of the age.

Additionally, this Greek word *apodeiknumi* provides us with another connection between the apostle and the king. *The Expanded Vine's Expository Dictionary* says, "The word is frequently used in the papyri of the proclamation of the accession of a king or the appointment of an official."[1] Paul, by using this word, is once again explicitly telling us that he is making the connection between the apostle and the king.

The Ministry Characteristics of the King

There are more than 2,500 Old Testament verses concerning kings. This overwhelming number gives us ample opportunity to properly examine this anointed one. Obviously, the few passages quoted here are highly significant. One of the most significant passages describing Israel's king is in the Book of Deuteronomy, written centuries before Israel's first king reigned.

It is significant that the Lord set rules in place for Israel's king even before Israel had a king. This fact should correct the erroneous idea that the establishing of the kings of Israel was a sinful rejection of God. God was not offended by the Israelites' desire for leadership. It was the "kind" of leadership that they wanted that offended God. What offended God in Israel's desire for a king was

---

1.   pg. 1023, Vine.

that they wanted a king *like the nations around them*. They had
forgotten that God had set them apart as a special nation. The Lord
had warned them of this, as recorded in the Book of Deuteronomy.
The characteristics listed were to make sure the kind of king that
Israel had was different from the other nations.

> *When you enter the land the Lord your God is giving you
> and have taken possession of it and settled in it, and you
> say, "Let us set a king over us **like all the nations around
> us**," be sure to appoint over you the king the Lord your
> God chooses. He must be from among your own brothers.
> Do not place a foreigner over you, one who is not a brother
> Israelite. The king, moreover, must not acquire great num-
> bers of horses for himself or make the people return to
> Egypt to get more of them, for the Lord has told you, "You
> are not to go back that way again." He must not take many
> wives, or his heart will be led astray. He must not accumu-
> late large amounts of silver and gold. When he takes the
> throne of his kingdom, he is to write for himself on a scroll
> a copy of this law, taken from that of the priests, who are
> Levites. It is to be with him, and he is to read it all the days
> of his life so that he may learn to revere the Lord his God
> and follow carefully all the words of this law and these de-
> crees and not consider himself better than his brothers and
> turn from the law to the right or to the left. Then he and his
> descendants will reign a long time over his kingdom in Is-
> rael* (Deuteronomy 17:14-20).

This long passage instructs us in several points about Israel's
kings.

Selected by Revelation of God's Choice

The king was to be of God's choosing. The people of God were
to appoint only the man whom God had chosen. (It is here that we
see the ministry of the prophet to be sent to appoint and anoint
kings.) The Israelites were never to appoint a foreigner over them;

the king must be a brother Israelite. And he must not consider himself better than his brother Israelites.

This is also true of the apostle. The apostle must be selected by God and revealed and appointed to the ministry by the Church. He must be known by them. He cannot be a foreigner. The apostle must never think that his calling means he is better than others.

Avoidance of Accumulating Great Wealth and Power

The king was not to acquire great wealth in the form of silver and gold, military might through many horses, or seek political advantage through marriage to many princesses of other nations. The king was also not to send the people back to Egypt to acquire horses. This is another way of saying that the king was not to rely on the means and ways of the pagan kings around him to establish his kingdom, but rather he should know that the Lord would establish him through supernatural means.

The apostle likewise must not use his anointing and position to acquire great wealth. Although it is certain that a financial anointing is upon apostolic ministry, it must never be the primary function of the ministry. The apostle must never rely on the world's methods of finance or play politics to try to accomplish the will of God.

Submitted to and Humbled by the Word of God

The king was not to be an authority in himself. In fact, he was to be humbled, corrected, and instructed daily by a copy of the Law that he himself would copy from the priest. His divine authority as king was based upon his reverence for the Law of His God. His throne and his descendants would be established by God only if he obeyed the Word of God. Thus the king of Israel was to be very different from the pagan king who was a law to himself.

Likewise, the apostle must never extend his authority beyond the limits of God's Word. He must never seek to become the "lord" of another. His authority comes from the willing submission of those whom God has given him. He must trust God to establish him and never rely on the world's ways of control, such as creating fear in others. For those who are rebellious, he must trust God to judge and establish his authority where it is rejected. The apostle should exercise authority as a shepherd and never as a tyrant.

Another Warning About Kings

Another informative passage is found in First Samuel. In this passage, the Israelites demonstrated a lack of insight about their uniqueness as a holy nation by asking for a king *like the nations around them.* God spoke to Samuel, telling him to warn them about the practices of kings.

> *"Now listen to them; but warn them solemnly and let them know what the king who will reign over them will do." Samuel told all the words of the Lord to the people who were asking him for a king. He said, "This is what the king who will reign over you will do: He will take your sons and make them serve with his chariots and horses, and they will run in front of his chariots. Some he will assign to be commanders of thousands and commanders of fifties, and others to plow his ground and reap his harvest, and still others to make weapons of war and equipment for his chariots. He will take your daughters to be perfumers and cooks and bakers. He will take the best of your fields and vineyards and olive groves and give them to his attendants. He will take a tenth of your grain and of your vintage and give it to his officials and attendants. Your menservants and maidservants and the best of your cattle and donkeys he will take for his own use. He will take a tenth of your flocks, and you yourselves will become his slaves. When that day comes, you will cry out for relief from the king you have chosen, and the Lord will not answer you in that day"* (1 Samuel 8:9-18).

Even after this warning, Israel still desired a king like the nations around them. Samuel appointed and anointed Israel's first king, Saul. This passage is instructive, for it tells us what the potential activity of the king was to be. It is clear that God was saying to them that He was a better King than any human ruler could be because He had not done these things. It is also clear that He was not condemning these things as sinful, but was stating in a practical sense what the custom of a king would be. We will continue to examine the characteristics of the king from this passage.

Recruiting the Best People

The king would recruit the best and most gifted people to serve him in all the arenas of life: military, agriculture, domestic, design and creation of weapons, and so on. In a similar but spiritual manner, apostles will attract the best people by the anointing that is upon them. Those who are functioning in fivefold ministry gifts and who are in fellowship with God will find themselves drawn to apostolic ministry. Indeed, it is a characteristic of the apostolic ministry to find the other gifts in submission to that ministry. Apostles need not recruit as the Old Testament kings did; God will send and attach other gifts to their ministry. The apostle, however, must be ready to share the ministry, open doors, and encourage those whom God gives him. Should he not make room for them, God may give them to someone else with a greater vision of the Body of Christ.

The King Will Take the Best Land

The Old Testament king would rule over all the land and would take the best land for himself. He would set his subordinates over the land, as the passage above and as the following verse reveals.

Solomon also had twelve district governors over all Israel, who supplied provisions for the king and the royal household. Each one had to provide supplies for one month in the year (1 Kings 4:7).

Apostles are team ministry persons. They will establish as many works and acquire as many properties as God allows. They are interested in a continual increase in ministries being released and works established. They are organizers and expect cooperation in ministry. They generally expect their subordinates to succeed and usually grant much ministerial freedom to those associated with them. They recognize the uniqueness of every ministry God raises up and do not try to force them into their mold.

They see the rule of the Lord established wherever their subordinates are successful. They are successful in their own minds and hearts because their subordinates are successful. The apostle will think in terms of territory that he can bring under the authority of the Lord Jesus Christ through local churches and ministries.

Collection of Taxation

The king levied and collected a ten-percent tax on the whole harvest by means of his subordinates. (This would be beyond the 10 percent already required in the tithe that the priesthood received.) In like manner, apostles seem to have the Midas touch. The apostle operates in an anointing and faith for finances. He does not need to "fleece" the people of God; to do so would short-circuit that which God would establish. The supernatural anointing on the apostle touches the Church and releases finances. The supernatural anointing on apostolic ministry is revealed when the apostle refuses to reveal the financial need to the Church at large, yet God speaks to individuals to provide the specific amount. The apostle "taxes" the Church in prayer before the Lord, and the Lord releases the finances to the apostle. Many apostles seem to be independently prosperous and do not need the Church to supply for them. The money they receive goes to finance the Kingdom of God's spiritual warfare campaigns.

The King Will Reign by Righteousness and Justice

God foretold that the king would become more powerful and the people less powerful—to the point of potential slavery. The king would have the right to command the people, even against their wills. The Book of Judges makes an interesting comment to this attribute of the king. In the context of the Book of Judges, however, it is a negative comment about the unrestrained and sinful lives of the people despite their freedom from a king.

In those days Israel had no king; everyone did as he saw fit (Judges 17:6).

One of the king's important responsibilities in the area of rule or command was to *maintain justice and righteousness*.

*Praise be to the Lord your God, who has delighted in you
and placed you on the throne of Israel. Because of the
Lord's eternal love for Israel, he has made you king, **to
maintain justice and righteousness** (1 Kings 10:9).*

The king also would make righteous judgments and rulings in
matters of dispute. The following example illustrates King Solomon functioning in this role. It is the famous situation in which
two women argued over who was the mother of a particular baby.
Solomon created a situation through which the real mother was revealed. He then commanded:

*Then the king gave his **ruling**: "Give the living baby to the
first woman. Do not kill him; she is his mother." When all
Israel heard the verdict the king had given, they held the
king in awe, because they saw that he had wisdom from
God to **administer justice** (1 Kings 3:27-28).*

The apostle, likewise, must maintain justice and righteousness
within the Church. The apostle has duties of administering discipline if necessary. This is not a function that a godly leader would
desire, but one that is absolutely necessary to maintain standards
of holiness and integrity within the Church. There are several examples of the administration of apostolic discipline within the
Church in the New Testament. Sometimes this discipline was supernatural; other times it seems to have been more natural. In any
case, it was the apostle exercising authority as a king to exile (ex-
communicate) someone or to execute a penalty, sometimes death,
supernaturally.

The King Conducts Warfare

In First Samuel chapter 8 we see hints that the king would assume primary responsibility for the nation in the arena of warfare.
This clearly occurred shortly after Saul became king.

*After Saul had assumed rule over Israel, he fought against
their enemies on every side: Moab, the Ammonites, Edom,
the kings of Zobah, and the Philistines. Wherever he turned,
he inflicted punishment on them (1 Samuel 14:47).*

The king was the primary agent in recruiting, training, building, and preparing the strategy for the conduct of warfare. This ministry function has a lineage from Moses and Joshua through the Judges, and was the domain of the king. The Scriptures note that this was not unique to Israel. King David's own troubles with sin began with the fact he was neglecting the kingly duty of leading warfare.

*In the spring, **at the time when kings go off to war,** David sent Joab out with the king's men and the whole Israelite army. They destroyed the Ammonites and besieged Rabbah. **But David remained in Jerusalem** (2 Samuel 11:1).*

Warfare is an important function of the apostle. It is so important that this work will deal with it in greater detail later. The apostle must be equipped and ready to live in continual warfare with demonic and evil angelic forces.

Three More Characteristics

In the following passage, when all Israel at last recognized David's call to be king, three more characteristics of the king's ministry were revealed.

"In the past, while Saul was king over us, you were the one who led Israel on their military campaigns. And the Lord said to you, 'You will shepherd My people Israel, and you will become their ruler.' " When all the elders of Israel had come to King David at Hebron, the king made a compact with them at Hebron before the Lord, and they anointed David king over Israel. David was thirty years old when he became king, and he reigned forty years (2 Samuel 5:2-4).

The Extension of Rule by Divine Intervention

This passage reveals that the godly king was promoted by God in various ways: extension of his kingdom over all the tribes of Israel, defeat of his domestic enemies, defeat and extension of his kingdom over foreign adversaries. The obedient apostle can expect ongoing extension of his ministry through spiritual victories, the saving of the lost, the healing of the saved, and releasing them into ministry. The disobedient apostle, however, can expect trouble in the form of his spiritual enemies making advances into realms already claimed and won for the Lord.

The godly and divinely obedient king could expect God's supernatural fulfillment of His promises. The promises of God to David in his childhood that he would be king were slowly fulfilled by God without David resorting to the unrighteous and wicked ways of pagan kings. Only by patient endurance was David eventually to sit on the throne of all Israel.

The obedient apostle likewise can expect his authority to be established slowly by God. He must not get ahead of God. He must walk before His God patiently and with endurance. If he is truly an apostle, God will make it evident in His perfect timing. The developing apostle has nothing to prove. He must not try to prove His calling to anyone. He must not seek to become more in men's minds than God has given him presently in the spiritual realm. This would be to court disaster, for he has only the grace for what God has actually given him. He must let God reveal his calling to others. The enemy will tempt the developing apostle to turn to men's ways of promoting themselves. If the developing apostle yields to this temptation, he will short-circuit God's ways of revealing him supernaturally at the right time and to the right persons. This important truth was also discussed in the earlier chapter dealing with the characteristics of the apostle and how we may identify a true apostle.

The King Maintains Relationships With the Elders

The king was to maintain a proper relationship with the elders of Israel, which included a proper relationship with the priesthood and prophets of Israel. He was to recognize and never usurp their ministries by means of his power. He needed to hear their words of wisdom and guidance in all matters. He was to support them by all means and place them in roles equal to their gifts and callings by God. For instance, we read in First Kings:

Azariah son of Nathan—in charge of the district officers; Zabud son of Nathan—a priest and personal adviser to the king (1 Kings 4:5).

Godly kings always allowed the prophets and priests of Israel access to themselves.

Likewise, the apostle is a man who appreciates all the gifts of the Body of Christ. He is open to other ministries. The apostle is not a law unto himself. He must rule by the consent of the governed despite his call from God. He must hear the wisdom that God has given to others. They will often have the pieces God has not given to him. The word of the Lord will come to him from God's New Testament prophets as well as in his personal prayer. He must hear the wisdom and feel the heart God has given to His pastors concerning the flock. God will make him dependent upon them, and they will be dependent upon him as well.

The King Must Reign Like a Shepherd

The king was to lead the people as a shepherd led his sheep. This was God's desire for King Saul.

> *"In the past, while Saul was king over us, you were the one who led Israel on their military campaigns. And the Lord said to you, 'You will **shepherd** My people Israel, and you will become their **ruler**' "* (2 Samuel 5:2).

God's desire for a king that would be a shepherd did not change with David.

> *" 'My servant David will be **king** over them, and they will all have one **shepherd**. They will follow My laws and be careful to keep My decrees' "* (Ezekiel 37:24).

The apostle likewise must have a shepherd's heart if he is to truly rule as God ordains. He can never look to the world's leaders, but he must be like his King, the Lord Jesus Christ, who is and ever shall be the Chief Shepherd.

Summary of Chapter Seven

The Old Testament godly king is a type of the New Testament apostle. While types have their limitations, much can be learned about the apostolic ministry by careful study of the ministries of the godly Old Testament kings. The Old Testament tells us that the godly king of Israel was not to be like the kings of the nations around Israel. The Old Testament king was to be selected by the revelation of God's choice. He was to avoid accumulating great wealth and power. He was to be submitted to and humbled by the written Word of God. The king would recruit the best people to be in service to him, and would take the best land for himself. He would collect taxes from the people for his own support and for the military defense of Israel. He was to reign by righteousness and justice always. The king conducted warfare against the enemies of God. The godly and obedient king could expect God to extend his rule by supernatural means—including intervention in warfare. God expected the king to maintain proper respect and relationships with the godly elders of Israel, i.e. the prophets and priests. Finally, the godly king was always to rule as a shepherd, unlike the tyrants who ruled other nations. Each one of these aspects of the godly king provides insights into the correct functioning of the apostolic ministry.

Chapter 8

Saul and David as Types of Apostles

God Hides Apostles Until the Proper Time

Earlier in this book, we discussed two different ways in which apostles have been hidden. First, they have been hidden by tradition and doctrinal misunderstanding. Second, apostles have been hidden through inconsistent translation of the Greek word *apostolos* into terms other than *apostle*. There is a third way that apostles can be hidden from the world and from the Church; God first calls the apostle in a private, hidden way and later reveals him in public. If the apostle is faithful, then God will continually promote, reveal, and increase him.

Lesson in Leadership for Apostles

In the lives of the godly kings of the Old Testament, the apostle can find many lessons of leadership and many types of his ministry. A study of the method that God used in elevating his first selections as kings of Israel provides insight into how He calls, reveals, and elevates His apostles today. Since our interest is in seeing the apostolic ministry reestablished in the present time, looking at the ministry of kings after they were well-established would miss the point. So we will examine Saul and David as examples of individuals God established as kings. David's example is especially interesting, since he is also an example of a young king in the process of replacing an older king.

God's Selection of Saul as King of Israel

Saul's selection as Israel's first king began with a curious set of events. Through these events, the Lord set the stage for Saul to learn of his selection by God. The events began with Saul being sent unsuccessfully by his father to search for some lost donkeys.

Now the donkeys belonging to Saul's father Kish were lost, and Kish said to his son Saul, "Take one of the servants with you and go and look for the donkeys." So he passed through the hill country of Ephraim and through the area around Shalisha, but they did not find them. They went on into the district of Shaalim, but the donkeys were not there. Then he passed through the territory of Benjamin, but they did not find them. When they reached the district of Zuph, Saul said to the servant who was with him, "Come, let's go back, or my father will stop thinking about the donkeys and start worrying about us (1 Samuel 9:3-5).

Saul was ready to give up searching for the donkeys. But his servant had another idea, one that placed Saul right into the path of God's sovereign plan for him. Saul's servant was aware that the prophet Samuel lived nearby and suggested that they seek guidance from him.

But the servant replied, "Look, in this town there is a man of God; he is highly respected, and everything he says comes true. Let's go there now. Perhaps he will tell us what way to take" (1 Samuel 9:6).

God Reveals His Selection to the Prophet Samuel

Still interested in hearing what the prophet might say about the donkeys, Saul proceeded into the town with his servant to seek the prophet Samuel, unaware that the Lord had already spoken to the prophet Samuel about him the day before.

Now the day before Saul came, the Lord had revealed this to Samuel: "About this time tomorrow I will send you a man from the land of Benjamin. Anoint him leader over My people Israel; he will deliver My people from the hand of the Philistines. I have looked upon My people, for their cry has reached Me." When Samuel caught sight of Saul, the Lord said to him, "This is the man I spoke to you about; he will govern My people" (1 Samuel 9:15-17).

Samuel did not immediately reveal God's words concerning Saul. Instead Samuel ate a feast with Saul. He informed Saul supernaturally that the donkeys had been found and that he need not be concerned about them any longer. As Saul began to leave to return home, Samuel told Saul that he had a message for him from God. However, he waited until they were alone to state the message.

As they were going down to the edge of the town, Samuel said to Saul, "Tell the servant to go on ahead of us"—and the servant did so—"but you stay here awhile, so that I may give you a message from God" (1 Samuel 9:27).

Samuel Anoints Saul King in Private
Samuel eliminated the only other possible human witness to the next set of events by having Saul send the servant ahead. Samuel then obeyed the Lord's command and anointed Saul as king over Israel. No one else knew of it, however; only God, Saul, and Samuel knew of this anointing.

Then Samuel took a flask of oil and poured it on Saul's head and kissed him, saying, "Has not the Lord anointed you leader over His inheritance?" (1 Samuel 10:1)

Saul Receives Divine Signs of His Selection
Samuel then revealed that God would give Saul a number of signs that He was with him. This was to assure Saul of the accuracy of Samuel's word to him, demonstrating it was from God. Samuel supernaturally predicted these things to Saul:

When you leave me today, you will meet two men near Rachel's tomb, at Zelzah on the border of Benjamin. They will say to you, "The donkeys you set out to look for have been found. And now your father has stopped thinking about them and is worried about you. He is asking, 'What shall I do about my son?' " Then you will go on from there until you reach the great tree of Tabor. Three men going up to God at Bethel will meet you there. One will be carrying three young goats, another three loaves of bread, and another a skin of wine. They will greet you and offer you two loaves of bread, which you will accept from them (1 Samuel 10:2-4).

These supernaturally predicted events should have been enough for any man to know that his call from God was sure, but Samuel added more:

After that you will go to Gibeah of God, where there is a Philistine outpost. As you approach the town, you will meet a procession of prophets coming down from the high place with lyres, tambourines, flutes and harps being played before them, and they will be prophesying. The Spirit of the Lord will come upon you in power, and you will prophesy with them; and you will be changed into a different person (1 Samuel 10:5-6).

Samuel explained that these events were to be signs that God was with Saul as king.

Once these signs are fulfilled, do whatever your hand finds to do, for God is with you (1 Samuel 10:7).

God Has Instructions for Saul

Samuel then gave Saul additional instructions. He was to wait in Gilgal for Samuel for one week. On that day God fulfilled all the signs Samuel had predicted.

"Go down ahead of me to Gilgal. I will surely come down to you to sacrifice burnt offerings and fellowship offerings,

but you must wait seven days until I come to you and tell you what you are to do." As Saul turned to leave Samuel, God changed Saul's heart, and all these signs were fulfilled that day (1 Samuel 10:8-9).

Samuel gave Saul these additional specific instructions. He was to wait in Gilgal for Samuel to come and offer a sacrifice. The passage does not clearly indicate when Saul was supposed to do this. However, it is clear that it was not to be immediately. Later we are told it was at the time appointed by Samuel. A number of other important events transpired before Saul meets Samuel at Gilgal.

Saul Is Supernaturally Revealed to All Israel

God worked inwardly in Saul and outwardly in objective supernatural signs, as Samuel predicted. However, Samuel apparently did something Saul did not expect, something Samuel did not tell Saul he was going to do. Before the commanded meeting at Gilgal, Samuel brought together all the people of Israel to reveal to them their new king.

Samuel summoned the people of Israel to the Lord at Mizpah and said to them, "This is what the Lord, the God of Israel, says: 'I brought Israel up out of Egypt, and I delivered you from the power of Egypt and all the kingdoms that oppressed you.' But you have now rejected your God, who saves you out of all your calamities and distresses. And you have said, 'No, set a king over us.' So now present yourselves before the Lord by your tribes and clans" (1 Samuel 10:17-19).

After reminding them that their desire for a king was offensive to Him, God began to reveal His selection by choosing a single tribe, a single clan within that tribe, and a single man within that clan. Most translators use a more literal translation than used here by the New International Version. These translators have used the word *chosen*; however, most other translations use *chosen by lot*, which tells us of the actual method of choosing Saul. This is, of course, a supernatural revelation of Saul to Israel since he had already been anointed by Samuel.

When Samuel brought all the tribes of Israel near, the tribe of Benjamin was chosen. Then he brought forward the tribe of Benjamin, clan by clan, and Matri's clan was chosen. Finally Saul son of Kish was chosen. But when they looked for him, he was not to be found. So they inquired further of the Lord, "Has the man come here yet?" And the Lord said, "Yes, he has hidden himself among the baggage" (1 Samuel 10:20-22).

Saul himself was obviously unprepared for this revelation. He hid himself during this selection process, but God revealed his location. Samuel then announced Saul as the king of Israel.

They ran and brought him out, and as he stood among the people he was a head taller than any of the others. Samuel said to all the people, "Do you see the man the Lord has chosen? There is no one like him among all the people." Then the people shouted, "Long live the king!" (1 Samuel 10:23-24)

After this revelation to the people, Samuel explained what having a king would mean to the people of Israel.

Samuel explained to the people the regulations of the kingship. He wrote them down on a scroll and deposited it before the Lord. Then Samuel dismissed the people, each to his own home. Saul also went to his home in Gibeah, accompanied by valiant men whose hearts God had touched (1 Samuel 10:25-26).

Not All Israel Believes or Accepts Saul as King

Saul returned home accompanied by those valiant men whom God gave him. However, not everyone was pleased with Saul's selection as king. In fact, they were already critical of him. They apparently were not convinced about him, completely ignorant of God's selection of him in spite of the events and Samuel's presence.

> *But some troublemakers said, "How can this fellow save us?" They despised him and brought him no gifts. But Saul kept silent* (1 Samuel 10:27).

It is reasonable to suspect that every man of God will have his troublemakers, those who reject and despise him regardless of the level of his anointing. If Jesus had His critics, it is reasonable to expect that we will also. God's apostle must remain patient as God establishes his rule.

Saul as a Type of the Apostle

Saul was anointed king over Israel in private. Each apostle's call comes privately. Generally few know of it other than God and the apostle. Even if there are human witnesses, they are generally few and do not influence others about the call in the beginning.

For a period of time the apostle will be given signs that will confirm what God is doing in his life. These signs last only for a season and will precede the actual ministry of the apostle by years, possibly decades. Once the apostle is convinced of his call, the signs will generally cease, but on occasion God may remind His servant of what he is being prepared for.

When the time comes, the apostle will be supernaturally revealed to the Church. The Holy Spirit will select him, witness to others about him, and anoint him with power. This may also be a season of grace that lasts several years before its completion.

Some believers will receive the apostle's call by faith. Others will reject it or simply seem apathetic about it. In any situation, the apostle must function with the persons God has given and not seek to prove his apostleship to those who disbelieve. The fellow Christian who rejects his apostleship is God's problem, not the apostle's problem. God has an answer for His apostle—it lies in spiritual warfare.

The Spirit Anoints Saul to Lead Israel in Battle

This was not the final element of Saul's installation as king. It was only a short period of time before an additional series of events revealed to Israel that God had indeed given them a king. An Ammonite leader with an overwhelming military force challenged one of Israel's cities, Jabesh Gilead, setting the stage for a further revealing of their king.

> *Nahash the Ammonite went up and besieged Jabesh Gilead. And all the men of Jabesh said to him, "Make a treaty with us, and we will be subject to you." But Nahash the Ammonite replied, "I will make a treaty with you only on the condition that I gouge out the right eye of every one of you and so bring disgrace on all Israel."...When the messengers came to Gibeah of Saul and reported these terms to the people, they all wept aloud* (1 Samuel 11:1-2,4).

The Ammonite leader agreed to the covenant, but with a severe stipulation: He would gouge out the right eye of every man. Not wanting to comply with this indignity, the men of Jabesh Gilead sought help from the other Israelites. The news of these events reached Saul's city of Gibeah. Saul heard the bad news after returning to the city from the field.

> *Just then Saul was returning from the fields, behind his oxen, and he asked, "What is wrong with the people? Why are they weeping?" Then they repeated to him what the men of Jabesh had said. When Saul heard their words, the Spirit of God came upon him in power, and he burned with anger* (1 Samuel 11:5-6).

This was the first time that Saul had displayed anything remotely resembling kingly qualities. Although he had been anointed with oil and called by God to this ministry, it was then that the power of the Holy Spirit anointed him to be the king of Israel. His God-given anger against the enemies of Israel moved him to action.

> *He took a pair of oxen, cut them into pieces, and sent the pieces by messengers throughout Israel, proclaiming,*

"This is what will be done to the oxen of anyone who does not follow Saul and Samuel." Then the terror of the Lord fell on the people, and they turned out as one man. When Saul mustered them at Bezek, the men of Israel numbered three hundred thousand and the men of Judah thirty thousand (1 Samuel 11:7-8).

As Saul exercised his authority as king of Israel, he was given assistance by the Lord. He mustered the warriors of Israel at Bezek and led them successfully in a battle against the Ammonites.

The next day Saul separated his men into three divisions; during the last watch of the night they broke into the camp of the Ammonites and slaughtered them until the heat of the day. Those who survived were scattered, so that no two of them were left together (1 Samuel 11:11).

God Strengthens His King Through Victory in Battle

This complete victory raised people's confidence in Saul's reign as king. In fact, they began to want to destroy those who had been his detractors before.

The people then said to Samuel, "Who was it that asked, 'Shall Saul reign over us?' Bring these men to us and we will put them to death" (1 Samuel 11:12).

In not allowing them to kill these men Saul demonstrated godly qualities. He also gave God proper credit for the victory.

But Saul said, "No one shall be put to death today, for this day the Lord has rescued Israel" (1 Samuel 11:13).

Saul Receives a Third Recognition as King

However, Samuel took the opportunity of this victory to bring the people into a new and deeper commitment to their king. This was the third occasion on which Saul was acknowledged as king: The first time was in private with Samuel, the second time was through lot in front of all Israel, and the third time was at Gilgal after this military victory.

*Then Samuel said to the people, "Come, let us go to Gilgal
and there reaffirm the kingship." So all the people went to
Gilgal and confirmed Saul as king in the presence of the
Lord. There they sacrificed fellowship offerings before the
Lord, and Saul and all the Israelites held a great celebra-
tion* (1 Samuel 11:14-15).

Similarly, the apostle will find that as God leads him into spiritual warfare, he will be able to increasingly muster the forces of
the Church. With each spiritual victory over principalities, his rule
and authority will become more firmly established.

Another Military Test of Saul

Not long after these events, Saul found himself in another military crisis. The Philistines had become enraged by his son
Jonathan's military success against them and intended to put an
end to it. They assembled an impressive military force.

*The Philistines assembled to fight Israel, with three thou-
sand chariots, six thousand charioteers, and soldiers as
numerous as the sand on the seashore. They went up and
camped at Micmash, east of Beth Aven* (1 Samuel 13:5).

This military force produced great fear in the army of Israel.
Some soldiers began to desert even before the battle had begun.

*When the men of Israel saw that their situation was critical
and that their army was hard pressed, they hid in caves and
thickets, among the rocks, and in pits and cisterns. Some
Hebrews even crossed the Jordan to the land of Gad and
Gilead. Saul remained at Gilgal, and all the troops with
him were quaking with fear* (1 Samuel 13:6-7).

Saul's Faith Fails and He Sins Against the Lord

The time the Lord had commanded through Samuel had arrived, and Saul was awaiting the promised arrival of Samuel at
Gilgal. The seven days passed, and Saul began to experience de-
sertions from within his own force. In a panic himself, Saul made
a critical decision:

He waited seven days, the time set by Samuel; but Samuel did not come to Gilgal, and Saul's men began to scatter. So he said, "Bring me the burnt offering and the fellowship offerings." And Saul offered up the burnt offering. Just as he finished making the offering, Samuel arrived, and Saul went out to greet him (1 Samuel 13:8-10).

This was, of course, in disobedience to the word of the Lord and to the Scriptures. Only those from the tribe of Levi could make the prescribed offerings to the Lord. Samuel arrived shortly after Saul made the offering and questioned Saul:

"What have you done?" asked Samuel. Saul replied, "When I saw that the men were scattering, and that you did not come at the set time, and that the Philistines were assembling at Micmash, I thought, 'Now the Philistines will come down against me at Gilgal, and I have not sought the Lord's favor.' So I felt compelled to offer the burnt offering" (1 Samuel 13:11-12).

Samuel Corrects the Erring King

This was not Saul's real reason; he simply lost his faith and allowed impatience to take over. Saul was only trying to excuse himself from responsibility for his sin. He had made a practical, but unbelieving, political decision to keep the allegiance of the people. He felt that he had to take things into his own hands and could not count on the word of the Lord.

"You acted foolishly," Samuel said. "You have not kept the command the Lord your God gave you; if you had, He would have established your kingdom over Israel for all time. But now your kingdom will not endure; the Lord has sought out a man after His own heart and appointed him leader of His people, because you have not kept the Lord's command" (1 Samuel 13:13-14).

Although it was 40 years before this prophecy was completely fulfilled in Saul's life, his kingdom still did not endure. His son,

Jonathan, died the same day he did. His decline as a king began with this disobedience and continued, increasing throughout his life. The next few chapters of First Samuel show Saul again disobeying the command of the Lord through Samuel. As a result of this disobedience, the anointing of the Holy Spirit left Saul and began to be upon the young man David.

The apostle who begins well can end as poorly as Saul did. In his rule for God the apostle must continue to look to God and not to human methods. Failure will come only through disobedience to God. Temptation will come to trust in man's methods and forget how God blessed and worked for him in the beginning, yet he must remain faithful or "his kingdom will not endure."

David's First Anointing as King

The life of David serves as an excellent example of the waiting, growth, development, and ministry of the apostle. David's three anointings as king over God's people illustrate the faithfulness of God to fulfill His promises to His servants.

It wasn't long after Saul's sin and rejection as king that the Lord sent Samuel to anoint His next selection for king of Israel. We cannot forget that the former king, Saul, was still sitting on the throne when this happened.

The Lord said to Samuel, "How long will you mourn for Saul, since I have rejected him as king over Israel? Fill your horn with oil and be on your way; I am sending you to Jesse of Bethlehem. I have chosen one of his sons to be king" (1 Samuel 16:1).

Samuel did not reveal to Jesse what his intentions were or why he had come to his household. And after Samuel consecrated the household and sacrificed to the Lord, he began to consider which of Jesse's sons God had chosen. He wrongly thought God had chosen the eldest son. But God corrected him by inwardly speaking to him these words:

But the Lord said to Samuel, "Do not consider his appearance or his height, for I have rejected him. The Lord does not look at the things man looks at. Man looks at

the outward appearance, but the Lord looks at the heart"
(1 Samuel 16:7).

After seeing all the sons Jesse presented, Samuel concluded that God had not chosen any of these sons. He asked Jesse if he had other sons:

So he asked Jesse, "Are these all the sons you have?" "There is still the youngest," Jesse answered, "but he is tending the sheep." Samuel said, "Send for him; we will not sit down until he arrives" (1 Samuel 16:11).

David, the youngest son, was tending the sheep. Samuel commanded that he be sent for. When he arrived, the Lord spoke to Samuel and chose David to become the anointed king.

So he sent and had him brought in. He was ruddy, with a fine appearance and handsome features. Then the Lord said, "Rise and anoint him; he is the one." So Samuel took the horn of oil and anointed him in the presence of his brothers, and from that day on the Spirit of the Lord came upon David in power. Samuel then went to Ramah (1 Samuel 16:12-13).

The anointing of the Holy Spirit came on David that day and began to prepare him for his future ministry for the Lord. He was the anointed king over Israel, but few knew of it. It was dangerous information; if Saul had known of this, he would have killed both Samuel and David. This anointing by Samuel was a divine fact, yet it was still private and secret. The anointing's effect, however, was not secret and began to manifest in David. David's anointing caused him to begin to be victorious over the enemies of the Lord. This drew a following of mighty men, and eventually brought Saul's jealousy and murderous hatred. In spite of this, David showed himself to be a man of character, and he never lifted his hand against Saul, the Lord's anointed. Despite his earlier calling, he never tried to install himself as king.

The man with an apostolic calling must not assume that because he is called he is prepared to assume that which God has called him to, even if he is a minister of some experience. One of the most serious problems in the local churches of America is that a man with a calling is allowed to assume an important position in the Church without first being trained and tested over a period of years. It is hard to name an individual of any merit from the Scriptures who did not go through years of preparation before assuming his ministry. God will not forget His calling of His man. The day will come for His installation of His man. Temptations will come to play the politician and not wait upon the Lord; however, yielding to them will have painful and possibly tragic results.

David's Second Anointing as King

Eventually God sent David, his family, and the men who had been given to him to the city of Hebron in Judah. God was setting the stage for a partial fulfillment of the promises He had made to David more than a decade before.

> *In the course of time, David inquired of the Lord. "Shall I go up to one of the towns of Judah?" he asked. The Lord said, "Go up." David asked, "Where shall I go?" "To Hebron," the Lord answered. So David went up there with his two wives, Ahinoam of Jezreel and Abigail, the widow of Nabal of Carmel. David also took the men who were with him, each with his family, and they settled in Hebron and its towns* (2 Samuel 2:1-3).

After David's settling in Hebron, God had the men of Judah anoint him king of Judah. This one tribe responding to David in this fashion was a partial fulfillment of the promises of God. He was beginning to see what God had spoken to him when he had been anointed by Samuel as a youth.

> *Then the men of Judah came to Hebron and there they anointed David king over the house of Judah* (2 Samuel 2:4a).

David was 30 years old when he became king over Judah. The past decade had been extremely dangerous and difficult for him. Saul had persecuted him, and he had been forced to live without a real home. Saul died by his own hand shortly before David was declared king of Judah. David had kept himself innocent in that matter and allowed God to deal with His servant Saul in His own time. David had not publicly opposed Saul or been responsible in any way for his demise. God began to replace Saul by David in His own timing. Now David had become king over one of the tribes.

The apostle must keep himself innocent in regard to already established ministries. He does not need to "steal sheep" or to injure the other servants of God in his domain. If he is truly an apostle, he can afford to be patient. The anointing will draw "one tribe" of believers and servants of God to his side. God will faithfully establish the promise of the apostle's call.

David's Third Anointing as King

After seven-and-a-half years as king of Judah, the Lord installed David over all the tribes of Israel. We could say that his rule over Judah was on-the-job training for ruling over all God's people.

All the tribes of Israel came to David at Hebron and said, "We are your own flesh and blood. In the past, while Saul was king over us, you were the one who led Israel on their military campaigns. And the Lord said to you, 'You will shepherd My people Israel, and you will become their ruler.' " When all the elders of Israel had come to King David at Hebron, the king made a compact with them at Hebron before the Lord, and they anointed David king over Israel (2 Samuel 5:1-3).

It is noteworthy that God had previously trained David and that he was already known to the elders of Israel. He had been tested and was known by them. These items should be lessons to the called but not yet functioning apostle. It is not too much to expect God to promote His apostles slowly and train them in the same manner by not putting too much responsibility upon them right away. There is no question that the apostle who waits upon the Lord will be ready for the challenge. The man who thrusts himself into this ministry may find himself quickly overwhelmed and without the resources to endure for long.

Summary of Chapter Eight

Both Saul and David had a secret calling of God in common. In each case no one knew of it, except a few people. They both had a time in which God prepared them to assume their calling. In Saul's case this time was rather short. In David's case it was much longer. Both received supernatural witness to their callings by the Lord. Saul received signs and his supernatural selection by lot in front of all Israel. David had his victory over Goliath and victories over each enemy he faced. Saul's faith and character failed when the going got rough. David, on the other hand, waited upon the Lord in faith and in the midst of a multitude of difficulties, and eventually he saw the final fulfillment of the promises of the Lord.

The modern apostle should find much instruction in the example of the godly kings of Scripture. Both the successes and failures of the kings will instruct the "crown prince" apostle. The functioning apostle will be able to avoid the failures of many of God's servants in order to glorify Jesus the Apostle and reveal Him as King of kings and Lord of lords through his obedient and humble ministry.

Book Three

Apostles and the End Times

Chapter 9

Apostles and the Unity of the Church

Jesus Prays for Supernatural Unity

In chapter 17 of the Gospel of John, the Lord Jesus prayed to the Father for all believers, for those who existed in that day and for us. This passage has been commonly called the High Priestly Prayer. He asked the Father to make us one in the same manner that He and the Father are one.

> *My prayer is not for them alone. I pray also for those who will believe in Me through their message, that **all of them may be one, Father, just as You are in Me and I am in You. May they also be in Us so that the world may believe that You have sent Me*** (John 17:20-21).

The Church being *one* in the same manner as the Father, Son, and Spirit are united will reveal to the world that Jesus Christ has been sent from God. Should there be any doubt that Jesus is praying for this supernatural kind of unity of believers, in the next verse He repeats some of these same truths. The Lord Jesus prays that we "*may be one as We* [Jesus and the Father] *are one*." He prays that the Church might be *brought to complete unity.* When this complete unity is evident, the world will know that the Father sent Christ.

*I have given them the glory that You gave Me, that **they
may be one as We are one: I in them and You in Me. May
they be brought to complete unity to let the world know
that You sent Me** and have loved them even as You have
loved Me* (John 17:22-23).

It is unthinkable that the Holy Spirit would record this prayer
of the Lord in John's Gospel if the Father did not intend to answer
it. Indeed, the Father will powerfully answer this prayer near the
end of the age. God's answer for the unity of the Church of Jesus
Christ will happen increasingly through the ministry of the last
apostles. As all good members of a local church must be in loving
fellowship and in submission to their pastor, all Christian ministers will find a true and needed shepherd in the apostle God will
give them. All true local churches will eventually be related, submitted, and accountable to individual apostles functioning in their
God-given fields.

Apostles themselves will be related, submitted, and accountable to other apostles and to the individual church that sent them.
A season is coming when God will gently guide all His listening
and obedient servants into loving relationship, fellowship, and
submission to apostles. Each fivefold minister will have an individual God-given apostolic covering. Each apostle will have a
team of ministers whom God has entrusted as a stewardship to
serve with him. Each apostle will find himself loving, relating,
and submitting to other apostles. Out of this will come a practical unity of the Church. The servants of God will be protected
from the schemes of the enemy by genuine and humble submission and love. Out of this unity will come great anointing to
evangelize the lost and to defeat evil prince spirits that hold
multitudes in bondage.

Apostles Appoint Elders Over Churches

This is one of the clearest functions of the New Testament
apostle. This is revealed throughout the Book of Acts and a few
references in Paul's letters. The apostle is the only ministry that the
New Testament reveals may appoint elders or overseers over the

Church.[1] In his letter we also see Paul instructing the young apostle Timothy as to the qualifications for overseers and deacons.[2] Timothy needed to know these things since the function of an apostle was to appoint local leadership. Appointing the local pastoral authorities (elders or overseers) over the local churches reveals the apostle's continuing authority over those churches.

When an apostle has established a new work in a given locale, it has grown to sufficient size, and some individuals have sufficiently matured, the apostle will appoint elders to shepherd the people of God through the Holy Spirit's direction. In other words, the elders he selects become the pastors of the congregations. These men are often the fivefold ministry team that was given to the apostle by God for that particular locale. The apostle continues to exercise apostolic authority through these pastoral elders, and they remain accountable to him. After selecting these men, the apostle moves on to another work of planting or visits one of the previous works he has established. He may take part of the team that was given to him in other locations to help establish the next new work.

Accountability to the Church Sending Them

The apostle himself sets the example for his elders through his submission and accountability to the local church that sent him. It is a clear principle of the apostolic ministry that an apostle is sent from a particular church and remains accountable to that particular church. In other words, although the apostle may be an apostle to those churches he plants and supervises through elders, he is not in authority over the church that sent him as an apostle. He submits to the apostle, senior pastor, and other elders of that local church. This is a wonderful protection for the apostle. If he properly maintains this connection to his spiritual family, he will always have somewhere to go for personal counsel and encouragement in the midst of difficulties. If he has maintained an open and honest

1.   Acts 14:23; Titus 1:5.
2.   1 Timothy 3.

fellowship with his spiritual family, they will also be able to tell when he needs loving correction.

Submission Is Essential; Obedience Is Conditional

God's authority over us is unlimited and unconditional, but all appointed authority is limited and conditional. God's servants are limited by the Scriptures and the consciences of their subordinates. The submission of the apostle to his spiritual family, or any believer to an apostle or some other authority, is likewise limited. No one should ever expect a lockstep obedience in a matter without first giving serious consideration of the will of God. Adherence to the Scriptures and the dictates of conscience are protections to subordinates. No human authority, apostle or otherwise, should ever ask a subordinate to violate either the Scriptures or their conscience.

In practice, there may be times when a subordinate and an authority cannot agree on God's will for the subordinate. In those cases, it is possible for a subordinate to maintain a properly submitted attitude toward the God-given authority and yet not obey him in a particular matter. However, nothing should be done hastily or without serious deliberation and prayer for a better solution.

Disobedience to God-given authority is always a serious matter and must not be a function of rebellion, impatience, or the unbelief that God is somehow unable to get through to those in authority. Quite the contrary is true. God will get through to whomever He wishes to get through to when He wishes to get through to them! Praying and waiting for the authority to agree is often part of God's process of preparation for ministry. Although occasionally a situation may arise in which an apostle or elder must be disobeyed in order to obey the Lord, this cannot be the rule. It should be an extremely exceptional situation. Let us only disobey when a serious issue of the will of God is involved and we have honored the authority by consulting and appealing to them on the issue over a period of time.

Should no place of agreement be found after waiting patiently and prayerfully, then the subordinates may have no other choice than to disobey the human authority in order to obey the Lord.

However, great care must be exercised not to damage the relationship with the authority. If the relationship with the human authority is broken in the process, then a seeking of restoration should follow in the future, even if the issue remains. The apostle still remains accountable to the Church authorities who sent him, regardless of the outcome of a single issue of obedience. The Lord will ensure that someone, either the subordinate or the authority, comes to see his error in the matter, repents, and asks forgiveness. Proper conditions of respect, relationship, and fellowship need to be maintained by both the authority and the subordinate.

We see a pattern of apostolic accountability in Acts 13, where Paul and Barnabas are sent by the church at Antioch; they are then accountable to this particular church that sent them.

> *From Attalia they sailed back to **Antioch**, where they had been committed to the grace of God for the work they had now completed. On arriving there, they gathered the Church together and **reported all** that God had done through them and how He had opened the door of faith to the Gentiles. And they stayed there a long time with the disciples* (Acts 14:26-28).

Without this kind of humility and accountability, the apostle will not have the honest appraisal of people who know him and can see clearly his faults and the flaws in his ministry approach. He will surely fail without the honesty, love, and support of real friends who are not dazzled by the miracles found in his ministry.

Because of the present lack of understanding of this ministry, there are perhaps individuals in our day who are apostles who have not been sent according to this pattern and who have no one in particular to submit to. This creates a clear weakness in their ministries, and they should seek the Lord for grace to find a group of ministers who will acknowledge their apostolic ministry and provide oversight to them in practical ways. Without this protection from the deceptive methods of the enemy, the Lord may not be able to use His apostle to his full capacity. To think otherwise is a sure indication that the apostle does not yet understand the full extent of the enemy's power and proudly overestimates his own wisdom. This apostle needs to make a study of the multitude of ministries in our time that started strongly and ended poorly to see the error of his perspective.

Accountability to Other Apostles

There are those who consider apostles to be the head of the Church under Jesus and assume they are not accountable to anyone but Him. However, in the New Testament we find all the apostles of Scripture finding unity and making serious decisions only in direct consultation with each other. For instance, when Paul and Barnabas were in conflict with the "Judaizers," they consulted with the leaders of the church in Jerusalem and made a report of their ministry.[3] This was thought to have occurred around A.D. 50-51, some 14 years after Paul's conversion.

> *When they came to Jerusalem, they were welcomed by the church and the apostles and elders, to whom they **reported everything** God had done through them* (Acts 15:4).

Paul and Barnabas later continued their ministry based upon this decision, which was agreed upon by all the apostles and elders in Jerusalem.

> *As they traveled from town to town, they delivered the decisions reached by the apostles and elders in Jerusalem for the people to obey* (Acts 16:4).

This was not the last time Paul reported to or consulted with the apostles in Jerusalem. For instance, some eight years later, in A.D. 58,[4] Paul again consulted with the apostle James, the brother of Jesus and leader among apostles in Jerusalem.

> *The next day Paul and the rest of us went to see James, and all the elders were present. Paul greeted them and **reported in detail** what God had done among the Gentiles through his ministry* (Acts 21:18-19).

---

3.   pg. 340, Vol I, Schaff.
4.   pg. 346, Vol I, Schaff.

Paul himself tells us that he consulted with both Peter and James about the message he was preaching. Interestingly, the context of the passage is Paul's validation of his call as not being from men but from God. He shows us that there is nothing wrong in submitting oneself to the ministry of others. In fact, Paul validates the wisdom of doing so:

> *Then after three years, I went up to Jerusalem to get acquainted with Peter and stayed with him fifteen days. I saw none of the other apostles—only James, the Lord's brother* (Galatians 1:18-19).

> *Fourteen years later I went up again to Jerusalem, this time with Barnabas. I took Titus along also. I went in response to a revelation and set before them the gospel that I preach among the Gentiles. But I did this privately to those who seemed to be leaders, for fear that I was running or had run my race in vain* (Galatians 2:1-2).

Paul was able to leave this meeting with an assurance that he was preaching the same gospel as Peter and James. Their unity, understanding of each other, and acceptance of each other's apostolic ministries were established.

> *On the contrary, they saw that I had been entrusted with the task of preaching the gospel to the Gentiles, just as Peter had been to the Jews. For God, who was at work in the ministry of Peter as an apostle to the Jews, was also at work in my ministry as an apostle to the Gentiles. James, Peter and John, those reputed to be pillars, gave me and Barnabas the right hand of fellowship when they recognized the grace given to me. They agreed that we should go to the Gentiles, and they to the Jews* (Galatians 2:7-9).

It is apparent that no apostolic ministry will function successfully for long without the knowledge of and the trust of other apostolic ministries. Apostolic ministries that do not know each other well are sure to find conflict with each other over insignificant issues. It is God's intention for the unity of the Church to be reestablished through the love, mutual submission, harmony, and unity of these ministries. We must expect that mature apostles will be drawn to other mature apostles and find full acceptance, wisdom, and unity with them. Indeed, in the future the practical unity of the Church at large will depend upon the functioning of apostles with each other. God will bring His Church to submit to apostles in the future, and they will submit to each other—forming a practical unity in the Lord.

Some will not see the vision for unity and will think that they will lose their autonomy before the Lord by submission to others. This is extremely shortsighted. These ministries will experience the Lord's gracious discipline that will enable them to see their need for apostolic covering. Even though some will remain rebellious or fearful for a season while God patiently works with them, eventually submission will come or they will receive additional serious discipline from the Lord. God's discipline may even include allowing the rebellious servant of God to arrive prematurely at his heavenly rest. The true apostle must patiently wait for the Lord to deal with His rebellious or fearful servants. The apostle must continue to bless them even when his blessing is not returned.

Summary of Chapter Nine

The end-time purpose of God cannot be fulfilled without the unity of the Church. The evangelism of the lost and the defeat of evil prince spirits are dependent upon the practical unity of local churches. Functioning apostles are essential for the practical unity of the Church. Each apostle must be submitted and accountable to the individual local church that sent him. Each apostle must also be submitted and accountable to other apostles. As we near the end of the age, each true servant of the Lord will find God establishing him in loving relationship, fellowship, and submission to an apostle and the other members of an apostle's team. Each apostle will also find himself moved by the Holy Spirit to seek out submission and accountability with other apostles. Proper submission to compassionate authority produces unity, protection, and blessing that never violates the Scriptures or an individual's conscience before God.

Chapter 10

Apostles and Spiritual Warfare

Since this subject is complex, it is necessary to start at the beginning and speak generally on spiritual warfare. Then we will elaborate upon the specific functions of the apostle in spiritual warfare. This section lays out the particulars regarding the nature of the enemy's kingdom and the battle the apostle will be engaged in near the end of the age.

Man's Destiny Is to Rule the Earth

Initially the dominion of the world was given by God to Adam and Eve. By implication, this dominion was also given to their children and their children's children. However, this was before their disobedience to the word and will of God. God's words in Genesis reveal His plan for mankind:

*Then God said, "Let Us make man in Our image, in Our likeness, and let them **rule over** the fish of the sea and the birds of the air, over the livestock, over all the earth, and over all the creatures that move along the ground." So God created man in His own image, in the image of God He created him; male and female He created them. God blessed them and said to them, "Be fruitful and increase in*

*number; fill the earth and **subdue** it. **Rule over** the fish of
the sea and the birds of the air and over every living crea-
ture that moves on the ground* (Genesis 1:26-28).

Consider how the psalmist expressed this truth of man's dominion over the earth. Although lower, or lesser in power, than the
angels (translated as *heavenly beings*), God has set man to be the
ruler over the world.

*When I consider Your heavens, the work of Your fingers,
the moon and the stars, which You have set in place, what
is **man** that You are mindful of him, the son of man that You
care for him? You made him a little lower than **the heavenly beings** and crowned him with glory and honor. You
made him **ruler over the works of Your hands;** You put
everything under his feet: all flocks and herds, and the
beasts of the field, the birds of the air, and the fish of the
sea, all that swim the paths of the seas. O Lord, our Lord,
how majestic is Your name in all the earth!* (Psalm 8:3-9)

Yet we find other statements in the Scriptures declaring that
Adam gave this dominion up to Satan and his evil spirit princes, or
principalities. In other words, an evil fallen angel, Satan, replaced
the man, Adam, in dominion over the world. Understanding that
an angel, Satan, replaced a man is important to our discussion;
God is reversing this through spiritual warfare. Now it will be particular men, i.e. apostles, under the authority of Jesus Christ who
will war against and replace the demonic principalities that rule
over the earth. The present domination of the world by these satanic agents is clear. For instance, the apostle John tells us in his
first letter:

*We know that we are children of God, and that **the whole
world** is **under the control of the evil one*** (1 John 5:19).

This truth is further emphasized in Luke's account of the temptation of Christ in the wilderness.

*The devil led Him up to a high place and showed Him in an
instant all the kingdoms of the world. And he said to Him,*

"I will give You all their authority and splendor, for it has been given to me, and I can give it to anyone I want to (Luke 4:5-6).

Jesus does not deny or dispute the truthfulness of the devil's claim to the world. The devil tells the truth in partial form when it benefits his aims. The more complete truth is that the world belongs to God and was given to Adam and Eve and their descendants. However, because of their fall into the hands of the devil, he now controls it.

Christ, however, as the Second Adam, has defeated the devil, regained the authority, and now controls the world through believers who exercise this hard-won authority and power through the Holy Spirit. Therefore, Satan, fallen angels, and demons war against the true Church for dominion of the world.

When the devil says that the world has been given to him, this is an obvious reference to Adam's sin in the garden that gave the devil legal authority over the world. The devil now controls the world and influences the inhabitants within it. How does the evil one control the world? The following section seeks to answer that question.

Evil Prince Angels Control the World

Chapter 10 of the Book of Daniel provides some important insights into the nature of the spiritual world we live in. This passage begins with Daniel's seeking God with fasting and prayer for three weeks because he wanted insight into God's purposes.

At that time I, Daniel, mourned for three weeks. I ate no choice food; no meat or wine touched my lips; and I used no lotions at all until the three weeks were over (Daniel 10:2-3).

At the end of the 21 days, a dazzling angel appeared to Daniel:

I looked up and there before me was a man dressed in linen, with a belt of the finest gold around his waist. His body was like chrysolite, his face like lightning, his eyes like flaming torches, his arms and legs like the gleam of burnished bronze, and his voice like the sound of a multitude (Daniel 10:5-6).

The men with Daniel became afraid, even though they could not see the vision of the angel, and fled. Daniel was weakened from fasting. His reaction to the angel overcame him and he fell asleep. But he was awakened and strengthened by the angel's touch. Then the angel began to speak these words:

*He said, "Daniel, you who are highly esteemed, consider carefully the words I am about to speak to you, and stand up, for I have now been sent to you." And when he said this to me, I stood up trembling. Then he continued, "Do not be afraid, Daniel. **Since the first day** that you set your mind to gain understanding and to humble yourself before your God, your words were heard, and I have come in response to them"* (Daniel 10:11-12).

This is highly instructive and important information about spiritual warfare. First of all, Daniel's prayers were heard by God on the first day, yet no answer came for 21 days. The angel reveals why he had been unable to come to Daniel on the first day:

But the prince of the Persian kingdom resisted me twenty-one days. *Then Michael, one of the chief princes, came to help me, because I was **detained** there with the **king of Persia*** (Daniel 10:13).

The angel then reveals that the reason it took 21 days to reach Daniel with the answers he desired was that a fallen angel, the prince of the Persian kingdom, had resisted him those 21 days. The godly messenger angel then revealed to Daniel that he still would have been detained, but for the aid of one of the godly chief prince angels, Michael. The archangel Michael is referred to by name in a number of places in the Old and New Testaments.[1] Michael's aid

---

1.   Daniel 10:13, 10:21, 12:1; Jude 9; Revelation 12:7.

to this subordinate godly angel apparently allowed him to complete his mission of bringing God's word to Daniel. The angel revealed to Daniel what had happened and what was about to happen as he returned to Michael.

> *So he said, "Do you know why I have come to you? **Soon I will return to fight against the prince of Persia**, and when I go, **the prince of Greece** will come; but first I will tell you what is written in the Book of Truth. **No one supports me against them except Michael, your prince"*** (Daniel 10:20-21).

The angel provided further insight into the spiritual realm by describing what he had been doing as a *fight*. He also told Daniel that he must return to again "fight against the prince of Persia" and that another evil fallen angel, the prince of Greece, would apparently join the fray at that time. In other words, the angel gives us a picture of four angels engaged in conflict. The angel speaking to Daniel and Michael the archangel will be engaged in a fight with the evil angel princes of Persia and Greece. The evil prince angel over Greece was apparently dispatched to aid the evil prince angel over Persia. This evil prince angel's freedom to reinforce his neighboring evil prince angel in this battle is also enlightening.

Fallen Prince Angels Rule Countries for Satan

Daniel 10 reveals that Satan's kingdom is highly organized. The angel speaking to Daniel revealed that over the geographical areas that were described as Persia (present-day Iran) and Greece, fallen evil angels were ruling. These fallen angels were not ruling on the earth itself, but somewhere in between heaven and earth.

Some confusion is caused by the choice of the translators of many New Testament versions to use the singular *heaven* for the Greek word that is normally plural and should be translated *heavens*. This brings to mind Paul's statement in Second Corinthians 12:2 about the "third Heaven" where he saw things he could not put into words. Apparently it is this third Heaven that is actually what is meant by Heaven in most people's minds. This leaves, however, two more heavens to explain. The first heaven is what we normally speak of as the sky. It is the atmosphere around the earth. The second heaven is the area where fallen angels have taken up residence in between the earth and the third Heaven, where God dwells. From this position, they resist the extension of God's Kingdom on the earth. They oppose godly angels and try to keep them from accomplishing the will of God on the earth. They also resist the work of the Holy Spirit.

It is not hard to then apply this understanding and state with some certainty that over every land mass in the world, there is an assigned evil angelic prince ruling as a subordinate of Satan. Satan himself is described as the ruler of the kingdom of the air who is now at work in those who are disobedient.

*In which you used to live when you followed the ways of this world and of the **ruler of the kingdom of the air**, the spirit who is **now at work in those who are disobedient*** (Ephesians 2:2).

These fallen princely angels are often called "principalities." A principality is, of course, the realm of a prince. The King James Version uses the term *principality* in Ephesians 6:12. However, the New International Version has chosen to use the word *rulers* instead of *principalities*. The actual Greek word is *arche*. It is used in several places in reference to angels, both evil and righteous.[2] It is translated into a variety of words: *principality, ruler, power, authority*, and probably other words as well.

Satan, a finite being, cannot be everywhere at the same time, so he is obviously at work through his subordinates: evil angel principalities in the heavenly realms and demonic spirits on the earth. Paul tells us more about these princes, or rulers, when he describes our warfare.

2.   Romans 8:38; Ephesians 3:10; Colossians 1:16, 2:15; Titus 3:1; Jude 6.

*For our struggle is not against flesh and blood, but against the **rulers**, against the **authorities**, against the **powers** of this dark world and against the **spiritual forces** of evil in the heavenly realms* (Ephesians 6:12).

Paul gives us a defined order of these evil spiritual beings, which implies subordination—a hierarchy under these evil angelic princes or rulers. There are those who suggest that only Satan, his princes, and one level beneath the princes exist in the heavenlies by reason of the construction of this passage. The final two levels would then be comprised of earth-bound demons. Perhaps we could list them like this in order of authority and power:

In the heavenlies:
1. Satan (Lucifer or the devil)
2. Rulers (Greek: *Arche*, also translated as "principality")
3. Authorities (Greek: *Exousia* also translated as "powers")

On the earth:
4. Powers of world darkness[3]
5. Spiritual forces of darkness[4]

---

3. Robertson, *Word Pictures in the New Testament*, pg. 550. The Greek word for "powers" here is *arche*. Robertson suggests that since there is already an *arche* that was listed first in the passage (here as #2 and translated "ruler"), this *arche* is limited by the phrase "of world darkness." In other words, these are spirits limited to the world and not the air.
4. Robertson, *Word Pictures in the New Testament*, pg. 550. Robertson translates the particular Greek phrase here as "spiritual hosts of wickedness." He then says that there is no actual Greek word here for *hosts*, that literally the passage states, "spiritual things of wickedness." He also says that *wickedness* is the Greek word *poneria* and could be translated "depravity". This would mean that a literal translation could be "spiritual things of depravity." Since these are listed after "powers of world darkness," it would then follow that they are of a lesser authority and power and they are limited to the earth.

This strongly implies that there are evil angelic authorities seeking to dominate not only nations, but cities, ethnic groups, families, and individuals as well.

Three Levels of Spiritual Warfare

The able-bodied men of Israel were trained in warfare to be mustered in times of national crisis by their king. Of course, this function is now in the realm of spirit and not the flesh. All believers have personal spiritual enemies to overcome. Some have called these enemies assignments of the devil. Some have referred to them as familiar spirits. That is, these spirits have been with us all our lives and they are "familiar" with us to the point of knowing how to keep us in defeat. These demonic spirits work in various realms against the believer: unbelief, habitual sexual sins, ungodly character traits, sickness, false doctrine, and so on. They must be exposed and dealt with.

Not to practice personal spiritual warfare simply ensures defeat. Each believer must be able to fight by the Spirit and the Word in the spirit realm. Any aspects of our lives that are continually defeating us, that remain resistant to the Word of God and prayer, and that repeatedly fail to honor and glorify God, may be suspected to harbor an unseen enemy. *Level One* of spiritual warfare is learning to fight and defeat our own personal spiritual enemies.

During His earthly days Jesus spent a great deal of time ministering to others who were afflicted by demons. This is *Level Two* of spiritual warfare. We must help others to obtain victory over their personal enemies. In many cases, deliverance ministry will be needed. All believers should be equipped and ready to minister in this realm. It is absolutely essential that all fivefold ministers be experienced and willing to minister deliverance.

Level Three of spiritual warfare is to combat and defeat the evil principalities in the heavenlies. This is an apostolic responsibility requiring the mustering of the Church in a given area in God's timing and purpose. As we have already related, one of the apostle's functions is to lead God's people in warfare against principalities and powers.

Christ Has Won the Victory

There is no victory against evil spiritual forces without understanding that Christ has already won the victory. This is a confusing thought for many people, but it is very clear in Scripture. For instance, the following passage declares that Christ's purpose was to destroy the devil's work:

He who does what is sinful is of the devil, because the devil has been sinning from the beginning. The reason the Son of God appeared was to destroy the devil's work (1 John 3:8).

This passage indicates that Christ has already won the victory through His cross. The evil prince angels, powers, and authorities have been destroyed and disarmed by Him. Paul is in complete agreement with what John has told us. He tells us that Christ has "disarmed" the devil and his princes. Paul uses the picture of the "Roman Triumph," which is a parade of defeated enemies in chains.

*And having **disarmed** the powers and authorities, He made a public spectacle of them, **triumphing** over them by the cross* (Colossians 2:15).

The writer of Hebrews also agrees that the devil has been destroyed by Christ's death.

*Since the children have flesh and blood, He too shared in their humanity so that by His death He might **destroy** him who holds the power of death—that is, the devil* (Hebrews 2:14).

Christ's victory is certain and can never be undone by the devil; however, it is not effective until it is applied in faith and spiritual warfare.

Christ's Victory Must Be Applied; It Is not Automatic

Although Christ's victory is complete and final over the devil and his angels, it has not yet been completely applied. Christ's kingship and complete defeat of the enemy are not currently evident from the status of Christians or His acceptance as Christ by the general public. Many people are experiencing quite the contrary; the enemy is anything but defeated in their lives.

Christ's victory must be applied by the Holy Spirit in each individual life. The victory and power of the cross of Jesus must be applied to all situations. Christ's victory is only incomplete in its application. Paul told the church at Rome that this experiential victory will come soon:

> *The God of peace **will soon crush Satan** under your feet. The grace of our Lord Jesus be with you* (Romans 16:20).

The Church must defeat Satan through the scriptural means at our disposal: warfare prayer against principalities and powers, and casting out demons. Jesus encourages us to "tie up the strong man" and then "rob his house."

> *And if **Satan** opposes himself and is divided, he cannot stand; his end has come. In fact, no one can **enter a strong man's house** and **carry off his possessions** unless he **first ties up the strong man**. Then he can **rob his house*** (Mark 3:26-27).

We must *carry off Satan's possessions*; that is, all the unbelievers he has dominated within the world. Christ has died for all of them and redemption is theirs, but Satan continues to keep them blinded and bound. Spiritual warfare will set them free. We must bind the strongman, Satan, and carry off his possessions. A parallel passage in Luke reveals another powerful truth: *Someone stronger has attacked and overpowered Satan. Satan's armor has been taken away and the spoils are being divided up by Christ.*

> *When a **strong man**, fully armed, **guards** his own house, **his possessions are safe**. But when **someone stronger** attacks and overpowers him, **he takes away the armor** in which the man trusted **and divides up the spoils**. He who is not with Me is against Me, and he who does not gather with Me, scatters* (Luke 11:21-23).

Keeping in mind that the victory is already won, we must by faith apply the victory in warfare prayer, binding the enemy and then casting out demons.

No Victory Without Obedience

There is no plan of action against principalities and powers to displace them in a human sense. The only plan that will work is "to pray and obey." We may understand much, but knowledge will not bring the victory. Victory will not be initiated by us, except as we pray and stand on the Word of God in faith. Victory will come as the Holy Spirit initiates it, fulfills the promises of God, and ministers the victory that Christ has already won over these satanic agents.

The Holy Spirit initiated the battle with Satan in the wilderness, an event generally known as the temptation. The Holy Spirit led Jesus into the wilderness to be tempted by the devil. A great victory was won there when Jesus refused to yield. Luke's account says that Jesus entered the temptation "full of the Holy Spirit," but that He left it "in the power of the Holy Spirit." His miracles and power over demons were evidence that He was spoiling the strongman's house. His later crucifixion and resurrection released this same power and authority to those who would believe in Him. They, however, must each prayerfully win their victories using the means that He has provided: the Word, the Blood, and the Spirit.

Apostles Replace Evil Prince Spirits

The Church must trust the Holy Spirit to guide it through its God-appointed leadership and direct it about matters in the unseen realms. If the apostle is obedient to the Lord, the very fact of his apostleship, his rule over a particular area, will pit him against particular evil angelic and demonic forces. The apostle initially may not know exactly who and what his enemies may be, but he can be sure that they will know who he is. He will gain the ascendancy over them little by little until God directs a major thrust against them. God will grant a great supernatural victory to dethrone the enemies.

The apostle must obediently wait on the Lord, trusting that God will give him the initiative and the upper hand in matters of warfare. If he is obedient to the Lord he will remain on the offensive. Even in matters where he may feel under great attack, simple obedience and trust in the Lord will turn the tide and the victory will come. The intensity of the attack will testify to the power of the victory about to be manifested. The fact of his apostleship means that God is moving him toward displacing his demonic and evil angelic foes and spoiling their house. This spoiling will bring salvation to the lost, as well as blessing, deliverance, and spiritual freedom to the believers that are bound.

The obedient, patient apostle will displace foes one at a time until he displaces the "power" over the city or area in which he dwells. The obedient and enduring apostle will then slowly solidify the Lord's growing blessing over the area by continuing spiritual warfare "cleanup" campaigns to deal with lingering demonic strongholds. The Holy Spirit will direct the new spiritual assaults.

As a result of spiritual warfare, there will be a new sense of freedom in all the churches. This new freedom will be experienced even by those who are unaware of the spiritual battles going on. Even those who oppose the apostolic ministry will experience new freedom to obey the Lord. The enemy's influence will be drastically reduced. The devil's kingdom will be in disarray as his princes are defeated and displaced. The Lord will then spoil his house, and salvation will come to many as King Jesus reigns through the apostle, the fivefold ministers, and the submitted local churches by the power of the Holy Spirit.

The Warring King as a Type of the Apostle

As we indicated earlier, the ministry of the apostle parallels the ministry of the Old Testament godly king in many respects. Indeed, it can be said to be a type of the apostle. One important function of the king that is distinct and finds no other fulfillment in any other Old Testament ministry is that the king led Israel into battle against the foes of God. This function had been previously found in the judges of Israel, but the time of the judges ended with the installation of Israel's first king. The apostle, as his ministry develops, will lead the people of God against the specific principalities and powers controlling the area in which God has called him.

Apostles Displace Evil Princes

It might be some time before these tendencies and abilities develop in the life of the apostle. God has hidden these individuals from the Church and the world until the arrival of the right time to reveal them. However, as that time approaches, the mature apostle whom God has established over a particular area will begin to impact the area of his authority by the Word of God and the Spirit of God. This will come after God has gathered suitable fivefold ministry persons to the apostle, and after suitable prayer forces are mustered by the work of the Spirit through this man. It is possible and even highly probable that many believers and fivefold ministers will recognize the authority of an apostle by the work of the Spirit of God and initially not understand that the man is an apostle.

Eventually, as the victory of the Savior is applied and the strongman is bound, great victories will be won over the prince spirits of each geographical area. Their dark spiritual influence will be broken over the inhabitants of a particular geographical area, victory by victory. This influence will be replaced by the Spirit of God working through the authority of the Church led by an apostle. As the ruling demonic forces are conquered in Christ, individuals will be free to favorably respond to the gospel. Complete evangelism of a particular area is therefore highly dependent upon the church's recognition of the ministry of the apostle.

The Conflict Is Territorial

Every apostle will know their God-established place of rulership. That is the field God has assigned to them. It should be the ambition of every apostle for the gospel to be fully preached, with signs and wonders, throughout the territory God has assigned them. This will necessarily include deliverance ministry or casting out demons as a regular part of ministry. If unseating the prince demons is one of the objectives of the apostolic ministry, the deliverance of each individual from evil spirits will weaken the evil prince spirit over a particular area and contribute to his final downfall. Here is what Paul had to say about the field assigned to him and those associated with him:

> *We, however, will not boast beyond proper **limits**, but will*
> *confine our boasting to **the field God has assigned to us**, a*
> *field that reaches even to you. We are not going too far in*
> *our boasting, as would be the case if we had not come to*
> *you, for we did get as far as you with the gospel of Christ.*
> *Neither do we go beyond our **limits** by boasting of work*
> *done by others. Our **hope** is that, as your faith continues to*
> *grow, **our area of activity among you will greatly expand**,*
> *so that we can preach the gospel in the regions beyond you.*
> *For we do not want to boast about **work already done in***
> ***another man's territory** (2 Corinthians 10:13-16).*

It is evident that Paul knew the limits of his territory and acknowledged that God had given responsibility to other apostles in
other territories. Apostles must hear from the Lord as to what their
particular territory is and not overstep their boundaries.

The current Church and its organizations must yield to the
Word of God and become reestablished in unity in localities. God
will not tolerate the present state of disunity much longer. This
reestablishing of unity will not be accomplished by carnal means
or through the cleverness of leadership. It will be accomplished by
prayer and warfare. It will not require compromise of the truth, but
it will require humility, submission, and love on the part of the
leadership of local churches.

Our vision must include the unity of the faith in practical, local
terms. The present nature of the Church must not blind our eyes to
her future glory. Her fragmented present nature is evidence of her
unpreparedness to meet her Bridegroom. This must change in
practical terms. This, of course, will not be accomplished without
serious spiritual warfare led by apostles who set individuals and
churches free to join the fray against the principalities and powers
in each locality. We have yet to see all that God will do.

Summary of Chapter Ten

Adam, a man, gave up authority over the earth to a fallen angel, Lucifer. As a man, Christ suffered, died as the ultimate Sacrifice, and was resurrected to regain the authority over the earth for

men. Christ gave His blood to bring dominion over the earth back to men. Christ's victory is not automatic, but it must be applied in spiritual warfare against presently reigning prince spirits.

This warfare against the enemy is threefold. Level One of this conflict is the individual believer's warfare against his own personal spiritual enemies. Level Two of this warfare is every believer's responsibility (particularly those of the fivefold ministry) to help all believers become victorious over their spiritual enemies. Level Three of this warfare is an apostolic function requiring the mustering of local churches in unity against the evil prince spirits dominating localities. These defeated evil prince spirits submit to and represent Satan in these localities. These evil prince spirits will be defeated little by little, and they will be eventually dethroned by the warfare of the Church. In contrast, a man who is an apostle and submitted to Christ will now reign spiritually over that locality in place of the displaced evil prince spirit. The apostle achieves this through the work of the local churches submitted to him.

Chapter 11

Apostles, Angels, and the Church

Godly Angels and the Church

Information about angels is not lacking in the Bible. The New International Version of the Bible lists over 300 direct references to angels. The Old and New Testaments authoritatively declare that God has assigned angels to protect His people, both Israel and the Church. For instance, the Book of Revelation is addressed to the seven angels of the churches. Some believe that this reference to angels is really a reference to the human leaders, i.e., the pastors, of these various churches. Even though this may appeal to our logic, there is no strong scriptural justification for such a belief. It is an improper interpretative method to arbitrarily state that the same Greek word means *pastor* here, but means *angel* only a chapter later. If the word means *angel* throughout the rest of Revelation, is must mean that here.

Churches Protected by Angels

It is very reassuring to know that although the country we may live in and those who remain unbelieving may be dominated by the demons of a directing evil prince spirit, those who are committed Christians, knitted into local churches, are protected and aided by the godly angel assigned to those local churches. Some of these phrases are recorded from Revelation:

> *To the **angel of the church** in Ephesus write...* (Revelation 2:1).

> *To the **angel of the church** in Smyrna write...* (Revelation 2:8).

Five other local churches are listed in similar fashion.[1]

Not Every Church Is Protected by Angels

Every building that has a sign out front calling itself a church is not protected by angels. Nor is every body of believers organized to form a church protected by angels. In fact, it may be that only those churches that are divinely established by the true call of God experience angelic activity on their behalf. Churches that are established through the will of man, or human energy, are not necessarily protected by God. If God did not originate the church, then He is not responsible for it.

It is possible that many organizations we call "churches" and many men we call "pastors" are not truly such in God's eyes. Everyone may be perfectly sincere, and the grace of God may be operating in the lives of individual believers, and the organization may have all the trappings of a church; but if it was not established and planted by the Lord, it is not His local church and He is not responsible for protecting it.

The apostolic churches in cities mentioned in Revelation 2 and 3 enjoyed the ministry of these protective angels. Paul may have also made reference to the ministry of angels to apostolic churches. This reference has been the subject of much debate and conjecture; he refers to angels in connection to the sign women were to wear to signify their submission to the authority of their husbands.

---

1.   Revelation 2:12,18, 3:1,7,14.

*For this reason, **and because of the angels**, the woman ought to have a **sign of authority** on her head* (1 Corinthians 11:10).

It could be argued that the woman came under the protection of the angel of the Church through the sign of authority she wore on her head. In other words, by proper submission to her husband's authority she enabled the angel's ministry to her. By her obedience to the Word of God and her submission to God-given authority, God became responsible for protecting her from the work of evil angels and released the work of godly angels on her behalf. The same could be said of her husband's scriptural submission to his pastor and the pastors' submission to the apostolic authority.

We might speculate from these verses that angels are particularly active in the ministries of apostles and in the churches that are properly constituted under their authority. Angels may be particularly active today and in the future through moving individual ministries into relationship with these last apostles. There are numerous references to angels "gathering" people.[2] Perhaps godly angels are working to gather God's people under proper apostolic authority, and the covering of apostolic authority releases the power of the Spirit and of godly angelic ministry in greater measure. The converse must also be considered; the enemy is more active against churches that are not under apostolic authority.

Michael the Archangel

There are many more practical things that must be learned about our enemies and God's plan to defeat them. However, it is now appropriate to change the focus of this book from the realms of darkness to the Kingdom of Light. It is exceedingly encouraging to discover that the passage of Daniel examined earlier describes the archangel Michael as "your prince."

---

2.   For example, Matthew 12:28-30, 13:30,39,41-43, 22:10, 24:31; Mark 13:27; Revelation 14:18-19, 16:14.

But first I will tell you what is written in the Book of Truth.
*No one supports me against them except **Michael, your***
***prince** (Daniel 10:21).*

This phrase, "Michael, your prince" reveals that the archangel
Michael had a special relationship with Daniel. A few verses later
this angel tells Daniel more about the archangel Michael. He says,
"Michael is the great prince that protects your people," meaning
that Michael is the protector of the Jews.

At that time Michael, the great prince who protects your
people, will arise. There will be a time of distress such as
has not happened from the beginning of nations until
***then**. But at that time your people—everyone whose name*
is found written in the book—will be delivered (Daniel
12:1).

Michael seems to be attached to the Jews, not necessarily to
the land of Palestine. Since most events of importance involving
the Jews occur in Palestine, therefore, it would follow that Michael spends a great deal of time protecting in that region. However, we must note that the events described in this passage are not
occurring in Palestine, but where Daniel was living in the region
of ancient Babylon. The archangel Michael came to the aid of the
subordinate angel assisting this Hebrew prophet. To come to
Daniel's aid seems in keeping with Michael's assigned duties to
the Jewish people.

Another interesting point about Michael: This verse indicates
that he will have an important ministry in the period near the end
of the age, during the time of distress which is ordinarily called the
Great Tribulation. Michael will once again arise to war against evil
angels. The Book of Revelation also speaks of Michael's end-time
mission of victorious spiritual warfare against Satan and his evil
prince angels.

*And there was war in heaven. **Michael and his angels***
fought against the dragon, and the dragon and his angels

fought back. But he was not strong enough, and they lost their place in heaven (Revelation 12:7-8).

Angels Need the Church's Authority

Satan and his subordinates operate in opposition to and in violation of God's Word until a greater power enforces it upon them. In other words, Satan and his subordinates are unarrested spiritual criminals. Apart from the Church, Michael the archangel has no legal authority or power over Satan. Christ has won the victory over Satan through His cross and resurrection. He has given His authority to the Church, not to Michael and his angels. Michael and his angels await a time of unity and powerful prayer on the part of the Church to release them legally and powerfully against Satan and his angels. When the unified Church exercises her spiritual authority in prayer, godly warrior angels will be able to defeat Satan legally and evict him from the heavenlies. Satan and his prince angels are to be *hurled down to the earth,* as the next verse declares.

*The great dragon was **hurled down**—that ancient serpent called the devil, or Satan, who leads the whole world astray. He was **hurled to the earth**, and his angels with him* (Revelation 12:9).

This successful spiritual warfare of *hurling down Satan* is clearly related to the Second Coming of Christ. According to the next verse, *"Now have come"* those things that relate to Christ's coming Kingdom.

*Then I heard a loud voice in heaven say: "**Now have come** the salvation and the power and the **kingdom of our God**, and the authority of His Christ. For the accuser of our brothers, who accuses them before our God day and night, has been **hurled down**"* (Revelation 12:10).

The next verse in this passage declares how the Church enabled Michael the archangel to hurl down Satan. These believers overcame Satan by *the blood of the Lamb* and *the word of their testimony*. As the Church exercised her legal authority over Satan by the means of declaration of Christ's sacrificial victory on the cross, i.e., His shed blood for them, they overcame Satan and his evil prince angels.

> *They **overcame** him by the **blood of the Lamb** and by **the word of their testimony**; they did not love their lives so much as to **shrink from death*** (Revelation 12:11).

It is clear that this warfare against Satan and his evil prince angels will require the complete consecration of the Church to God's purposes. There will be those who will victoriously give up their earthly lives in the conflicts to come. They will not shrink from death and therefore cannot be defeated. The next verse reveals that Satan will not give up his domination of the world without fury against the Church.

> *Therefore rejoice, you heavens and you who dwell in them! But woe to the earth and the sea, because the devil has gone down to you! He is filled with **fury**, because he knows that his time is short* (Revelation 12:12).

Despite this fury, the Church has nothing to fear from Satan. He has been defeated by Christ already. As we near the end of the age, the last apostles and the local churches will now apply this defeat in increasing fashion to Satan and his angels. The Church will release the ministry of powerful godly angelic warriors against Satan and his angels.

Godly angels will protect God's servants on the earth until it is necessary for some of the servants of God to seal their testimonies with their deaths. We can be assured that the decision of when and how the earthly lives of God's people are to end does not belong to Satan. Only the compassionate Lamb of God has that wisdom and power over His people, and more importantly, only He has the power to resurrect them.

Summary of Chapter Eleven
The work of the archangel Michael and other godly angels is important to the ministry of the last apostles. Michael and other

angels are protecting the Church and battling on its behalf. Satan and his subordinates are spiritual criminals who are willing to operate in violation of and in opposition to God's Word. Godly angels, however, will not operate illegally or in violation of God's Word. Since authority over the earth has been won by Christ and given to the Church, these godly angels await the proper exercise of this authority by the Church. These godly warrior angels will defeat Satan's prince spirits in regions where the Church is unified under apostolic authority. As these evil prince angels are defeated one by one, Satan's control over the world is seriously weakened. Finally, in unified global spiritual warfare, the last apostles and the Church will confront Satan himself. As a result of this warfare, Michael and his godly angels will forcibly and legally evict Satan and all his angels from the heavenlies. Satan will be in a great fury during those days, and some believers will seal their testimonies by suffering death for their Savior. The final events of this warfare will take place during a period of great distress upon the earth, which is also called the Great Tribulation.

Chapter 12

The Last Apostles

Seventy-Two More Sent Forth

The Gospel of Luke records the Lord Jesus sending 72 others forth in the same manner that He sent the Twelve.

After this the Lord appointed seventy-two others and sent them two by two ahead of Him to every town and place where He was about to go (Luke 10:1).

The Lord sent them with words nearly identical to those He had spoken to the Twelve before sending them. As we previously discussed, the term *send out* in Greek is linguistically related to the word *apostle.*

*He told them, "The harvest is plentiful, but the workers are few. Ask the Lord of the harvest, therefore, to **send out** workers into His harvest field. Go! I am **sending you out** like lambs among wolves" (Luke 10:2-3).*

The 72 were commissioned by Christ in similar fashion to the 12 Apostles. They were given power to heal the sick as they preached the gospel of the Kingdom of God.

"Heal the sick who are there and tell them, 'The kingdom of God is near you' " (Luke 10:9).

Seventy or Seventy-Two Nations in the World

The reader who is familiar with this passage might have already noticed that the New International Version says that Jesus sent "72" disciples rather than "70." In some versions of the New Testament, such as the King James Version, the passage states "70." The reason for the discrepancy between these versions is that there is a minor textual variant concerning these numbers in various existing ancient manuscript copies of Luke's Gospel. In other words, some ancient manuscripts of Luke's Gospel state there were 70 sent, and others state there were 72.

Textual variants generally have little effect on interpretation. Only about one half of one percent of the New Testament is variant. In comparison with other works of ancient literature from that day, the New Testament is exceedingly certain. Most of the variants in the New Testament have to do with the spelling of specific names or the tenses of verbs. Very few actually affect how one might interpret a given passage of Scripture. However, this textual variant is different. It makes this passage exceedingly interesting, since in an unusual way it points us to the correct prophetic meaning of the numbers 70 and 72.

When this text was written there was a theological debate among Jewish religious leaders concerning how many Gentile nations existed. One group believed that there were 70 nations. The other group believed that 72 Gentile nations existed. The textual variant in this passage points directly to this debate. This variant points to Christ's desire to send apostles into all the earth. The Lord has used this variant to reveal His desire to use apostles to reach all the nations of the earth.

The Final Fall of Satan

The Lord's sending of the 70 or the 72 is a prophetic revelation of a time coming when the last apostles will be sent to all the nations of the world to engage all the fallen satanic angels in vigorous, and ultimately victorious, spiritual warfare. Through the united power of submitted local churches, these last apostles will defeat these evil prince spirits one by one and confront Satan himself in unified global spiritual warfare until he too falls. In the next verses, the Lord Jesus speaks of this fall of Satan. This is in clear connection with the ministry of the 72 and their spiritual authority over demonic forces:

> *The seventy-two returned with joy and said, "Lord, even the demons submit to us in Your name." He replied, "I saw Satan fall like lightning from heaven"* (Luke 10:17-18).

In the next verses, the Lord reinforces the victory of the 72 apostles by telling them of their authority to overcome all the power of the enemy.

> *I have given you **authority** to trample on snakes and scorpions and to **overcome all the power of the enemy**; nothing will harm you* (Luke 10:19).

Jesus would not have told them of this authority they had if He had not expected them to use it completely against the evil prince spirits and overcome Satan himself. Since it is clear that Satan has not yet been overcome completely, there is still more of this authority to be exercised. The last apostles will not hesitate to use this authority against the forces of evil in their localities. The successful harvest of all the souls God wants to redeem depends upon these last apostles defeating the enemy completely.

Jesus' Joy At Their Victories Over Demons

Although we need to continue to focus our attention on our victorious heavenly Lord and rejoice in our salvation rather than focus on evil, it is clear that the Lord rejoices over our victories through simple faith in Him.

> *"However, do not rejoice that the spirits submit to you, but rejoice that your names are written in heaven." At that time Jesus, full of joy through the Holy Spirit, said, "I praise You, Father, Lord of heaven and earth, because You have hidden these things from the wise and learned, and revealed them to little children. Yes, Father, for this was Your good pleasure"* (Luke 10:20-21).

There is an implicit warning in this passage. The wise and learned might not see what God is doing. Perhaps those who are unable to shed the unbelieving doctrines of the past will be captives in these battles. It will take "the faith of little children" for us to be victorious. We cannot expect that all believers will respond in the simple and pure faith required to accomplish the Lord's purposes at the very end of the age. However, the last apostles will be as little children when it comes to simple faith and obedience to the Lord. The Lord is preparing all the vessels He will need to accomplish His work at the end of the age. At the very end of the age, there will be a large company of apostles going into all the world and bringing about Satan's fall. In this the Lord Jesus rejoices.

When Christ's Enemies Are His Footstool

The Old Testament verse quoted most frequently in the New Testament is the first verse of Psalm 110. It is quoted five times in the New Testament, more than any other verse.[1] It is clear that the Holy Spirit wanted to focus our attention upon the following phrase that is common to all six of the references:

"Sit at My right hand until I make Your enemies a footstool for Your feet."

In this passage God the Father is indisputably speaking to the enthroned Lord Jesus Christ. It is a prophecy of things to come. The Father says that His Son Jesus will remain at His right hand until His enemies are made a footstool for His feet. In other words, Jesus will not return to the earth until all His enemies are defeated. When Christ's enemies are made His footstool, Christ will return for His Bride, the Church. The ministry of the last apostles and godly angels will accomplish this work.

Summary of Chapter Twelve

At the end of the age, God is once again sending His apostles into all the nations of the world. When these last apostles exercise

---

1.   Matthew 22:44; Mark 12:36; Luke 20:42-43; Acts 2:34-35; Hebrews 1:13-14.

a unified spiritual warfare through the submitted local churches, multitudes of godly warrior angels will be released in warfare against the evil prince angels. Satan himself will be weakened as one by one his evil prince spirits are defeated. Finally, in unified global spiritual warfare, the last apostles will confront and defeat Satan himself. In the last days of this warfare, a great harvest of souls will come into the Kingdom of God. When all of Christ's enemies have been made His footstool, He will return for His Bride, the Church.

Appendix A

Apostles, Bishops, and Elders

The Church's Tradition Hides Apostles

In most religious people's minds, the term *bishop* has come to mean something like a "pastor's pastor." In other words, the widely accepted view is that a bishop is an ecclesiastical leader with authority over other church leaders and over a group of churches located in a particular geographical area. In some cases today, particularly among Charismatic groups, it is not a geographical area that is being supervised by a bishop, but rather simply a group of churches that hold a particular theological view or practice scattered over a large geographical area. All such bishops are unscriptural, from a point of strict adherence to the New Testament. But this modern use of the word *bishop* is also not traditional. Exercising authority over multiple churches is clearly part of the scriptural role of the apostle. After careful examination of the passages where this word *bishop* is used, there is little doubt that the traditional understanding of this term is also incorrect and is, from a strict scriptural standpoint, a heresy.

Apostolic Succession

The Roman Catholic Church has propagated the erroneous idea that there has been an unbroken line of bishops descending from Peter and that they have "inherited," one after another, the authority of the apostles. This belief is not taught in the Scriptures, and it was not taught by the early Church fathers. It also cannot be proven historically. It is a later invention of the Roman Catholic Church. The authority of the apostle comes from God's call alone and not by the Church. The Church must recognize the authority of the apostle, however, in order for him to be effective in any real measure. The Church needs to acknowledge the call, but it is not the source of the authority. That is why it is necessary to thoroughly test any man's claim to this ministry.

Unwittingly Stealing the Role of the Apostle

In some cases, there are men who have the calling and ministry of the apostle who have also been given or accepted the title of *bishop*. This is unfortunate, but it is certainly not as destructive to the work of God as those who are not apostles but who are now considered to be bishops by the Church. The Church often desires to honor outstanding leaders by giving them this title. Some of these men are extremely and wonderfully gifted by God, but are not apostles. Perhaps gifted and mature evangelists, pastors, prophets, and teachers are tempted to receive a role and calling they are neither gifted for nor called by God to function in because of the desire of those who have been blessed by their ministry to promote them. These ministries will need great humility to acknowledge fledgling apostles as they develop within their own congregations and even more humility to embrace those whom God develops outside their congregations.

Some have even been bold, or rather arrogant, enough to give themselves the title of *bishop*. There are some who hold this title who clearly do not have apostolic ministries and have unwittingly usurped the authority and ministry of the apostle. In the Book of Revelation, Christ's meaning is clear regarding those who would claim this kind of authority over multiple churches without God's sending:

I know your deeds, your hard work and your perseverance.
*I know that you cannot tolerate wicked men, that **you have***

***tested those who claim to be apostles but are not, and
have found them false*** (Revelation 2:2).

It is absolutely necessary for the Church to test those who
claim to be apostles. Those who are apostles should be able to
show both the seal and sign of apostleship, as well as having the
other characteristics. We note that God gave Moses two distinguishing signs to prove God had sent him. So we also expect that
apostles will have the seal of fully functional churches that they
planted and the sign of regular creative miracles in their ministries.
Without both indicators, the servant of God will fail the most basic
test of apostleship. There are secondary tests that must also be applied to any person claiming apostleship today.

The acceptance of the title *bishop* causes confusion in the minds
of the people of God about apostles and bishops. It will be necessary for the Church, as she once again makes room for the ministry
of the apostle, to teach clearly the actual meaning of the word that
is translated "bishop" and how it is used in Scripture. Before we
continue this discussion, a word of warning is appropriate.

No Opposition to Bishops Desirable

Although this understanding, or rather misunderstanding, of
this word and ministry will need to yield to the proper understanding of apostles, it is absolutely essential that no carnal means
be used to oppose any man who is called a bishop. Even prayer
against another believer is carnal. Believers are to bless one another and pray to the Lord for each other. Should a Christian leader
be in error, he needs prayer for the Lord to increase his understanding and to strengthen his humility and willingness to correct
himself. Prayer against another believer is on the borderline of
practicing witchcraft and will certainly invite the enemy into the
situation. Public criticism of a specific ministry may damage the
work of God through such an individual.

We should not "lift our hand against the Lord's anointed."[1]
David's attitude toward King Saul should instruct us. He would

---

1.   2 Samuel 1:14.

not injure this man who was still on the throne and was a threat to his life. He patiently waited for God to fulfill that which He had spoken to him. If the man is being used of God, we should not stand in judgment of him. Instead we should patiently allow the Lord to correct and deal with His servant. This does not mean, however, that we should embrace this error or be silent about it. We must believe that God's servants will hear the voice of the Spirit and, when the time is right, shed this unnecessary title. We must also believe that if such men are not apostles, they will release the churches from this relationship.

Greek Word *Episkopos* Translated "Bishop"

The King James Version of the Bible translates the Greek word *episkopos* and its various forms as "bishop." The New International Version does not use the word *bishop* at all, adding to the confusion about this word. New International translators have chosen to use a different and better word, *overseer*, to represent this Greek word. These differences in translation help to obscure the fact that the King James word *bishop* is being seriously misused from a strict scriptural standpoint. It is understandable that the King James translators would have used this word, since bishops were part of that medieval historical scene in England and Europe. Already there were 1,000 years of perpetuation of this error and, unfortunately for us, they perpetuated the error in this translation by using the word *bishop*.

As Martin Luther, John Calvin, and others were raised up by God in the Dark Ages of Europe to be forces in the Reformation, they and others were the first to acknowledge the misuse of the term *bishop*. The Reformers correctly explained the relationship between these terms. The terms *presbyter* (or elder) and *bishop* (or overseer) in the New Testament denote the same office—with this difference only, that the first term originated from the synagogue and the second from the Greek communities; and that one signifies the dignity of the office, while the other the actual practice of ministry.[2]

---

2.   pg. 491-2, Vol I, Schaff.

Misuse of *Bishop* Has a Long History

This misuse has a long history, stemming back to the third century. In the third century this word *episkopos* came to mean the single leader of the Church over a given geographical area and was said to refer to the successors of the 12 Apostles. This misuse carried the erroneous idea that there were only 12 apostles, that all the apostles had died in the first century, and that the bishops were their successors. There is absolutely nothing in Scripture to validate this idea. Unfortunately, the writings of the latter Church fathers help pass this idea on to the modern Church.[3]

The equality and interchange of the terms *elder* and *bishop* continued until the close of the first century, as evidenced by the Epistle of Clement of Rome written about A.D. 95. The Didache reveals that the equivalent meaning remained evident even near the end of the second century. However, with the beginning of the second century from Ignatius onward, the two terms began to be distinguished from each other. In other words, during the second century, the term *episkopos* began to lose its scriptural meaning and be transformed into something else. During this time the term *episkopos* began to mean "a head of a congregation surrounded by a group of presbyters." Decades later it came to mean a "head of a diocese and successor to the apostles." The *episcopate* grew out of the "presidency" of the presbytery.

The Reformation churches, i.e. the Lutherans, the Presbyterians, and the pre-Reformation Anabaptists, rejected the erroneous idea of bishops leading the Church; however, they did not reestablish the correct order of apostolic ministry. The New Testament uses *bishop* very differently than this later, traditional understanding. We will now address five basic problems with this traditional understanding.

First Problem: Multiple Bishops in a Single Church

Using the New International Version, if we were to substitute the word *bishop* or *bishops* in every case of the word *overseers*,

---

3.   pg. 493, Vol I, Schaff.

the problem of the unscriptural historical and traditional erroneous use of the term *bishop* begins to emerge. For instance:

> *Be shepherds of God's **flock** that is under your care, serving as **overseers**... (1 Peter 5:2a).*

One of the first things we notice in this passage is that a plural form of *episkopos* is being used in reference to the particular singular church, the "flock," that Peter has written to. In other words, there are multiple overseers in a single church. This is exactly opposite to the traditional understanding. This usage is clear in other passages as well. For example:

> *...To all the saints...at **Philippi**, together with the **overseers** and deacons* (Philippians 1:1).

There were multiple overseers in one local church at Philippi. These references above clearly show that there were multiple *episkopos* in each church. Instead of this first-century understanding, however, the term has degenerated from its original meaning and come to mean exactly the opposite, i.e. a single bishop over multiple churches and over a given geographical area. It is unfortunate that many of those who honor God's Word and know His grace in ministry have chosen (often in sincerity, but still in ignorance) to perpetuate this false idea about church leadership.

Second Problem: *Bishop* Equal to *Shepherd*

It is fortunate that the New International translators used "overseers" in most passages for *episkopos*, as that is the actual meaning of the Greek word. As we carefully look at the verses below it becomes clear that *shepherd* and *overseer* are equivalent terms describing different characteristics of exactly the same ministry.

> *Be **shepherds** of God's flock that is under your care, serving as **overseers*** (1 Peter 5:2a).

In the Book of Acts more instructive information is found. For instance, this verse gives us the same information—that *shepherd* and *overseer* are different descriptions for the same ministry.

*Keep watch over yourselves and all the **flock** of which the Holy Spirit has made you **overseers**. Be **shepherds** of the Church of God...* (Acts 20:28).

From the passages above, we can see that overseers are told to be "shepherds of the flock." It is abundantly clear from these passages that the ministries of overseer and shepherd are equivalent. This is clearly a ministry within a local church, not a ministry with a larger geographical oversight over multiple churches. Again, this is exactly the opposite of the traditional understanding.

Third Problem: *Bishop* Equal to *Elder*

Paul, while addressing the elders of the church of Ephesus, concludes his instruction to them by calling them "overseers."

*From Miletus, Paul sent to Ephesus for the **elders** of the Church* (Acts 20:17).

In a verse that has been previously quoted, while still speaking to these elders from the Ephesian church, Paul uses *overseers* and also *shepherds* to describe these same elders:

*Keep watch over yourselves and all the flock of which the Holy Spirit has made you **overseers**. Be **shepherds** of the Church of God, which He bought with His own blood* (Acts 20:28).

These verses alone should establish that the present use of *bishop* is improper and unscriptural, as well as possibly detrimental and resistant to the restoration of the modern-day apostle to his God-given calling. However, there are more verses to deal with that show that this term is being seriously abused and misused.

Fourth Problem: *Bishops* Serve with *Deacons*

The office of the deacon is mentioned several times in relationship with overseers, which indicates the latter ministry's clear connection to the local church rather than an ecclesiastical authority over multiple churches as mistakenly thought today.

*Paul and Timothy, servants of Christ Jesus, To all the saints in Christ Jesus at Philippi, together with the **overseers and deacons** (Philippians 1:1).*

In this passage, the ministry of *episkopos* is connected with the ministry of the deacon. It is clearly a ministry found in the local church. The word is plural, which indicates that in the local church of Philippi there was more than one *episkopos*. Once again, Scripture contradicts the traditional understanding of this word. Within the traditional understanding of the concept of bishops, there cannot be more than one in a given geographical area. Clearly, the traditional understanding is wrong and must yield to the Word of God.

As we discover from the verse above, there were multiple overseers in one local church in Philippi, as well as multiple deacons. We also note that the qualifications of the overseer and the deacon are listed together in the same chapter in the Book of First Timothy. This again establishes the idea that these ministries are connected and both function in a single local church. The fact that Paul instructs Timothy concerning the qualifications of both the overseer and deacon indicates that Timothy's ministry as a young apostle was to appoint them.

Fifth Problem: Elders Are Appointed by Apostles Alone

We have established that the term translated *bishop* or *overseer,* and *elder* are equivalent. In the next few verses, we will establish that apostles alone appoint elders. Since this is the case, it becomes increasingly clear that the present-day bishop has unintentionally stolen this role from the apostle. In today's church, it is these unscriptural "bishops" who are setting elders in authority over local churches. This traditional structure is seriously wrong and needs to be corrected. From the pen of Luke, we discover that the apostles alone appoint elders.

*Paul and Barnabas **appointed elders** for them in each church and, with prayer and fasting, committed them to the Lord in whom they had put their trust (Acts 14:23).*

From the hand of Paul to Titus we see confirmation of this aspect of apostolic ministry.

*The reason I left you in Crete was that you might straighten out what was left unfinished and **appoint elders** in every town, as I directed you* (Titus 1:5).

For a man to accept the ministry of *episkopos*, or "overseer," from any source other than the ministry of a functioning apostle is unscriptural, since these are equivalent terms. It is clear that an apostle would never appoint a bishop to usurp his own ministry. He would, however, appoint an overseer to function with other overseers to care for a particular local church. Perhaps it would be better for the Church not to use the term *bishop* at all, since it is laden with centuries of misuse. The term *elder* has been misused as well, but it has not been completely corrupted from its actual meaning. We must recover the scriptural understanding of the apostle and the overseer, and for the sake of the Church put away the unscriptural ministry and title of *bishop*.

It is evident from just a simple look at these passages that all or at least the vast majority of those Christian leaders who have accepted a title of *bishop* did not receive it from apostolic ministry and have accepted a role that usurps the role of the apostle. For present-day bishops to acknowledge this error to the churches that respect them will be difficult, but necessary, to make room for apostolic ministry to come forth. Otherwise, the "old wineskin" will not be suitable to hold the "new wine" of the Spirit that will be poured out in the days preceding the coming of the Lord.

In some cases, it will not be difficult for the man of God to dispense with this title and to instruct those who look to him for leadership about the apostolic ministry over a short time. It will be for him a question of humility and love for the truth. In other cases, due to long tradition it may not be possible to do so without serious difficulties. In any case, the Lord will grant His servant grace to embrace the truth.

Historical Decline and Recovery of Apostles

Historically, the decline of the apostolic ministry occurred as the unscriptural role of bishops was embraced by the Church. Which came first, the decline of apostles or the rise of bishops is a matter of debate. However, it is not a matter of debate that the Church suffered greatly as a clear decline in its supernatural functioning occurred during that period. By the end of the fourth century, the unscriptural bishops were fully in control, and the Church was beginning to embrace the world. It entered a serious moral decline, and the thousand years of the Dark Ages began. For that thousand years the function of bishops did little to bring the Church out of the Dark Ages. There is no doubt that there were godly men who served as bishops; however, many were simply politicians who used religion to further their own ambitions and greed. In fact, it was a break from their unscriptural authority that began the Protestant Reformation and began to bring the Church back into the light of God's Word. Now, a new Reformation is needed among Evangelicals. We need to embrace all that God's Word reveals and to hold back nothing. A "new wineskin" of apostolic strength will be needed to hold the gracious amounts of "new wine" that the Lord wishes to pour out upon the Church in our day. Nothing less will sustain the revival God is bringing forth.

Scriptural Role of the Overseer

As we have already established, the actual role of the overseer is the role of the elder, which is generally correctly understood within the modern-day Church. An elder is a subordinate leader within a local church who functions with other overseers to take care of a local church. He is an elder because he exercises authority collectively in spiritual government over a local body of believers. The overseers function together under the leadership of a single apostle and possibly a senior elder. Together they seek to hear the Lord's word and will for a particular local church. The ministry of the overseer is clearly not a translocal ministry with oversight over many churches; that is the role of the apostle and not the bishop.

Perhaps it would be better to altogether dispense with the term *bishop*. It has been so strongly tied to traditional and historical misuse that its use will continue to perpetuate confusion and make the apostle's role more difficult. Perhaps we simply need to use *elder* or *overseer* to describe this local church ministry to avoid confusion. Outside of this section in this work, the term *elder* will normally be used to avoid confusion.

To the "Bishop" Who Is Actually an "Apostle"

There are those who presently allow others to call them "bishops" because of their reluctance to embrace their actual correct ministry name of apostle. Perhaps the Church needs to reassure them of our acceptance of what the Word of God reveals about this ministry. If they have the characteristics and call of the apostle, then they should be identified as apostles of the Church without hesitation or fear. There will surely be those who will misunderstand because of traditional teaching, yet to submit to their unscriptural understandings and perpetuate confusion is certainly a worse choice for any man of God who believes that the truth will set the Church free. For the man of God who is a "bishop," but is not an apostle, there is no alternative but to repent and refuse to usurp the ministry of another. Only the truth will set the Church free to become His Bride.

Appendix B

Questions and Answers

Why do some churches teach that the ministry of the apostle and miracles ended in the first century?

Since the Reformation, God has been restoring New Testament truths one by one. The Reformers rediscovered justification by faith and other biblical truths during their lives. However, they did not rediscover truths such as healing, miracles, and the ministry of the apostle. In fact, in reaction to the superstitions and abuses of the medieval Roman Catholic Church, the Reformers taught against miracles. The writings of the Reformers reflect their ignorance and sometimes hostility toward these important New Testament truths. Many modern Protestant churches reflect the limited understanding of the Reformers. These churches have continued to teach the cessation of miracles and the ministry of the apostle to our day. Confusion has increased as churches have built additional doctrinal schemes upon this faulty foundation.

Much of this confusion about apostles comes from a modern doctrine popular today among some (but not all) theological conservatives called Dispensationalism. This doctrine has been propagated in the United States since about the mid-1800's, and has been popularized by the widespread use of the commentary notes of the Scofield Reference Bible. Some modern teachers believe that Dispensationalist doctrines were originally taught primarily as a reaction to the false Mormon teaching that Joseph Smith was a prophet. Some of its tenets are accepted by nearly all Baptist churches, some Pentecostal and Charismatic churches, and a variety of other churches.

There are many godly persons who were taught and possibly teach Dispensationalism. Dispensationalism is not entirely wrong and that makes it all the more deceptive to the Church. What it says about God's willingness to save us from sin is correct. However, it is wrong in many of its expressions concerning work of the Holy Spirit, and some of its expressions about eschatology. It is very wrong in its pronouncements about the ministry of the apostle.

What is Dispensationalism?

Dispensationalism is a way of viewing the Scriptures and the history of the Church. Dispensationalism properly divides biblical history into specific dispensations, or eras, of the work of God. It properly notes that God has worked differently in various dispensations. However, where it begins to go astray is that it arbitrarily divides the Church age into dispensations. For instance, without scriptural authority to do so, it states that after Acts 10, God no longer gives the Holy Spirit the same way He did previously. In effect, the passages about the Holy Spirit given before Acts 10 are negated in this scheme and are no longer considered good for doctrine.

One popular way Dispensationalism divides the Church age into arbitrary dispensations is through the passage on the seven Churches in Asia in the opening chapters of the Book of Revelation. Dispensationalism imposes these seven churches on the last 1900 plus years of the Church Age, making each church represent a particular part of Church history. Of course, this leaves the negative Church of Laodicea for the last part of the Church age, just before the Second Coming of Christ. So those who hold this view believe that the Church will be primarily lukewarm and apostate at the coming of Christ like the Laodicean church. This view affects how these Dispensational Christians treat those who don't agree with them. They are expecting apostasy from those around them and react accordingly by rejecting believers from other "camps" with little provocation. There is nothing in these passages in Revelation that gives authority to apply them in this scheme. In fact, the fruit of such an application seems rather negative, producing an expectation of apostasy, weakness, and failure in the Church in the last days.

The Church age is only one dispensation, not several. What God did in the first century He will do now. However, God's conditions remain the same. Faith must be evident. Dispensationalism teaches the Church not to expect or believe that God will work as He did in the New Testament, and it effectively prevents faith to receive God's manifold blessings.

Other serious theological conservatives are often rejected by Dispensationalists. It seems that many Dispensationalists consider only other Dispensationalists to be conservative. The truth, however, is that through their doctrine Dispensationalists are able to dismiss large portions of Scripture as not relevant for today in a manner similar to liberal theology. The only real difference between liberal theology and Dispensational theology is that they disagree on whether the first-century supernatural phenomena revealed by the New Testament ever happened. The Dispensationalist believes that the New Testament is accurate, while the liberal does not. However, both agree that it is not happening today. Therefore the Dispensationalist, much like the liberal, undermines the Scriptures and faith. (Of course, the Dispensationalist does allow for conversion; but so do many liberals. Liberals simply debate the nature of the conversion.)

Conservatives who reject Dispensationalism can therefore be considered more conservative than any Dispensationalist, for they cannot reject anything in the New Testament as irrelevant.

What the New Testament reveals is relevant for today. It cannot be dismissed for any reason. A true conservative must submit his doctrine to the correction of the New Testament and not correct the New Testament with his doctrines.

Wasn't the reason for miracles and healing to establish the Church and the Scriptures?

No. It can be shown historically that this is false. Miracles and healing continued throughout the Church age. This doctrine of the "cessation of miracles" comes from doctrinal systems built on the erroneous idea that *extraordinary supernatural means were used to establish the Church in the first century, and those extraordinary supernatural means are no longer needed*. Thus, these doctrines teach that God's will for today is not really revealed by the New Testament, since it is a document of another dispensation. Christian leaders who believe this doctrine would never state it in that manner, but this is what the outcome of their teaching implies. Various passages and entire New Testament books are rejected as not being applicable or are cut up as being only partially instructive for today. The New Testament, according to these doctrines, is only interpreted correctly if we understand their teaching.

Some prominent Pentecostals have borrowed these erroneous ideas in regard to the ministries of the apostle and prophet while rejecting it in regard to miracles and healing today. They teach that apostles and prophets today, if they exist, are not the same as the apostles and prophets revealed in the New Testament. This is an inconsistent theology that says that the functions of apostles and prophets are not the same as they were during the New Testament age, but still accepts the evangelist and pastor as being the same.

The actual reasons for miracles and healing today are clearly revealed in the Scriptures. Miracles and healing validate the gospel. Miracles and healing reveal the goodness and grace of God. Miracles and healing are signs of the resurrection to come. Miracles and healing are Jesus being made manifest in His Church.

Aren't the ministries of the apostle and prophet foundational? Since the foundation has been laid, they are no longer needed.

This is another extra-biblical doctrine that has been borrowed from heavily by Pentecostals and Charismatics. The idea behind

) This statement assumes that God's establishing is complete and there is no more establishing to be done by God or the church.

the question is this: "God used extraordinary means to establish the Church and the canon of Scripture, and these means are no longer necessary." In this case the extraordinary means are apostles and prophets. The question assumes what is meant by the "foundation" is *the apostolic doctrine contained in the New Testament*, which has already been laid by the first apostles and prophets. However, it is clear that the writers of the New Testament were not calling the New Testament the "foundation," since it had not yet been completely written. The 27 books were not yet in a collected form at that time.

The word *foundation* is used fairly often in Scripture in various ways. It is used literally, as a building's foundation, and figuratively, in reference to laying or building a foundation by teaching or preaching Jesus and the Good News; but it is not used in reference to the documents of the New Testament.[1] It is *never used* in reference to the apostolic doctrine contained in Scripture. It is used to refer to obedience to Jesus' words in the Gospels and to Paul's preaching of the gospel.

This requires some clear thinking. There are those who have not seen clearly that there is a distinction between the New Testament and the gospel. The gospel, the message about Jesus Christ, is older than the New Testament. The New Testament contains the gospel in written form, but it also contains things that cannot be said to be the gospel. For instance, the Book of Acts contains a historical account of Paul's travels. These cannot be said to be the gospel. Some of Paul's letters address Church problems. These cannot be said to be the gospel, even though they are clearly related. It is possible therefore to preach the New Testament and not preach the gospel of Christ, which is evident from the sad state of the Church in some locales. The foundation therefore is not the

---

1.   Matthew 7:25; Luke 6:48-49, 14:29; Acts 16:26; Romans 15:20;
       1 Corinthians 3:10-12; Ephesians 2:20; 1 Timothy 3:15, 6:19;
       2 Timothy 2:19; Hebrews 1:10, 6:1, 11:10; Revelation 21:14,
       21:19.

New Testament, but it is the gospel that lays Jesus as the Cornerstone of the Church.

The preaching and teaching of the gospel, which reveals Jesus as the Cornerstone and builds on that foundation, must happen in each generation. Apostles and prophets are instrumental in getting the foundation laid in each generation and will be particularly instrumental in this role in the last generation before the coming of the Lord. They will become prominent again just before the coming of the Lord. They began the Church age in prominence, and the Church age will not end without their prominence again. Scripture is complete and foundations must be laid from it. However, Scripture is not the foundation, but rather Jesus Himself is our foundation.

Some have suggested that apostolic and prophetic ministries are different now since the foundation has already been laid. The idea that prophets and apostles must now build on a foundation that was laid in the New Testament era seems to me to be a very dangerous idea. It sounds suspiciously like apostles and prophets must now add something to the New Testament doctrine, since only the foundation has been laid. In other words, it implies apostles and prophets now are building something that the original apostles could not have foreseen, since they only had the foundation. This is another way of saying that the New Testament is incomplete and inadequate for today's needs. This belief will lead to serious error since it will not allow the New Testament to judge what is being built today. It also reduces these ministries from their scriptural authority to something less. The foundation revealed by the New Testament must be laid by faithful preaching and teaching and supernatural ministry in each generation and in each person's life.

What is the effect of rejection of apostles and prophets on the local church?

Rejection of these ministries effectively robs the Church of many of its best ministries and most of its spiritual power. Normally those who reject apostles and prophets are suspicious of practically anything supernatural occurring in the Church, with the exception of being converted to Christ. Often the prophetic and apostolic ministries God has equipped with gifts of revelation, healing, and miracles are viewed with serious suspicion. Unbelief about these ministries effectively robs God of showing His extravagant grace and prevents Him from being glorified in healing and miracles. Countless Christians have died prematurely or suffered needlessly because of their rejection of God's choice prophetic and apostolic servants and the message and gifts they can bring.

I have heard that these miraculous ministries are from the devil. How can I be sure that they are from God?

We must evaluate them from the Scripture. Unfortunately, some unscriptural teaching causes believers to reject any ministry that appears similar to a supernatural New Testament ministry as being "of the devil." This teaching produces churches very unlike those the New Testament reveals. It produces churches of supposedly correct doctrine, words, and explanations, but without any supernatural power like the New Testament Church. When persons trained in a church like this encounter an anointed New Testament ministry, they are often afraid of it, even though it is often more similar to the ministry revealed in the New Testament than the ministry they are accustomed to. We must not reject a ministry simply because it is supernatural. We must evaluate it on the basis of Scripture and the fruit that it produces. Is the ministry glorifying Christ? Are the ministers themselves Christ-like in character? Are people being saved, strengthened, confirmed, and encouraged by the ministry?

Wasn't Matthias wrongly selected by man and Paul selected by God to replace Judas?

Some will argue that Matthias was selected by man and not by God. However, there is nothing in Acts 1 or in any other passage that suggests that Matthias' selection ever was questioned by the apostles. Certainly Luke, who records these events for us many years after Pentecost, would have revealed the error if the Church leadership had determined Matthias' selection to be a mistake. However, this is not the case. Acts 1 is entirely positive in tone about Matthias, without one suggestion that his selection was a mistake. This selection was done prayerfully and by casting lots, which ensured that the selection was done by God.

Selection by lot has troubled some in the modern age, as it seems like gambling. The pagan philosophy behind gambling believes that chance or luck controls the universe. However, the apostles did not hold to a false world view that would allow chance to operate. They believed in a God who actually controlled the universe. They had prayed and expected God to make His choice—and He did. In the Old Testament there are many examples of God indicating His choice by this method.[2] To question selection by lot is to question numerous examples of Old Testament servants of God using this method of selection—including God's choice of Saul as the first king of Israel. This selection by lot was supervised by none other than one of the greatest prophets of Israel, Samuel.

Nothing in the Scriptures, Church history, the writings of the fathers, or anyone prior to the modern age has suggested that using this method was a mistake. So what is the motivation to find fault with Matthias? It is an important point of some doctrinal systems that there are only 12 apostles and they must make allowances for Paul. So these systems must discredit Matthias in order to fit Paul into their doctrinal scheme. However, it seems apparent that Paul himself did not hold this view, since he is our primary source of information about the other apostles called after Jesus' Ascension. Additionally, there is nothing in the writings of the Church fathers to substantiate that Matthias was ever rejected or seen in a negative sense.[3]

---

2.   Leviticus 16:8; Joshua 18:6,8,10; 1 Chronicles 24:31, 25:8; Nehemiah 10:34, 11:1; Jonah 1:7.

3.   pg. 254, Lockyer.

Wasn't Paul a special exception to the "rule of apostles"?

No. In Acts 13:1-2, we see Paul and Barnabas being called together as apostles, and they are listed together as apostles in Acts 14:14. Luke must have thought Barnabas and Paul's calls as apostles to be at least equal. Paul himself does not indicate any sort of special call. He puts himself on par with Barnabas in First Corinthians 9:6-7. In the New Testament Paul's apostleship is intimately connected to Barnabas' apostleship. Luke's account of the call of Barnabas and Paul in Acts 13 places Barnabas and Paul on the same level, and may even suggest Barnabas' prominence. It is evident from earlier passages that the Church had no problem accepting Barnabas, but had clear problems with Paul, both early in his Christian experience and later in his ministry.

The word order is also significant. Paul is placed after Barnabas in both passages, suggesting Barnabas' prominence in this stage of the Church's development. It is noteworthy that this prominence did not continue, at least as the biblical record shows. After Paul and Barnabas' disagreement and separation over John Mark, the Book of Acts never mentions Barnabas again, and certainly from the evidence of the biblical account and history, over the next few decades, Paul became the more prominent. Dispensationalism cannot make room for Paul and then arbitrarily forget Barnabas. However, this is exactly what it attempts.

There are those within the Church today who teach that Paul was somehow a special exception to the rule of apostles. This is a very illogical idea; it is saying that *an exception to a rule establishes the rule*. Quite the contrary is true: If you can find a clear exception to the rule, then the rule must be wrong as stated. If Paul is the exception to the rule that there were only 12 apostles and God never intended for there to be more, then the rule must be wrong. It is very wrong, for as we survey the New Testament, we find more than 20 apostles. These doctrinal systems want us to limit the number of apostles to 12 or a special 13 because Paul is undeniably an apostle. And though we note that Paul was greatly used in many profound ways, he is certainly only one of many apostles.

Paul himself tells us in Ephesians 4:7-11 that after the Ascension Jesus Christ gave gifts to men. He then lists five ministry gifts. We also note that the word *apostles* is plural in this passage. For these doctrinal systems, this constitutes another problem to deal with. According to their doctrine, there can be only one apostle called after the Ascension, and that must be Paul. So why would Paul use the plural in this passage if he were the only apostle called after the Ascension? In fact, why would he include apostles at all, since he would be the last? Obviously there would be additional apostles (plural) called after the Ascension besides himself. In fact, most passages that identify other apostles are found in Paul's writings. He evidently believed that there were others beyond the original 12 and himself. If he did not believe in other apostles, why would he use the same Greek word *apostolos* to describe both himself and them? These doctrinal systems must be wrong about apostles.

Wasn't Paul sent by God and the other apostles sent by the Churches?

*Paul, an **apostle**—**sent** not from men nor by man, but by Jesus Christ and God the Father, who raised Him from the dead* (Galatians 1:1).

Dispensationalism suggests that this verse indicates a difference between Paul and other apostles because Paul indicates that he was sent by God and not by man. This is a faulty thought about apostles. The correct thought is, *"All apostles are sent by God and not by man."* The Church simply acknowledges the sending. This is in accord with the basic definition of *apostle*. Paul is not a different class of apostle. He is not a member of the 12 apostles of the Lamb, and he is not superior to the apostles of the churches, as some teachers suggest.

Paul is not distinguishing himself above other apostles; rather he is simply defending his call to apostleship. He does this frequently in his letters. Historically, we know that he was under considerable attack from within the Church concerning his apostleship. Paul fought against others wanting to give him an inferior status. Now there are those in the Church who want to give him a superior status. Neither is correct.

Paul is in no way indicating a superior call to other apostles, such as Matthias. If we were to ask Paul if he believed other apostles such as Matthias, Apollos, and Barnabas were sent by God and not by man, without doubt, Paul would have affirmed their divine missions as well.

In First Thessalonians 1:1 and 2:6, Paul makes no distinction between himself, Silas, and Timothy. They were all apostles. There was no doubt to their differing maturity levels and of Paul's leadership among them, but still he makes no differentiation on the basis of their call to apostleship. They may have been inexperienced apostles in relation to Paul, but they were apostles nevertheless. We note also that he refers to all three of them as apostles of Christ, again contradicting the erroneous teaching that some are apostles of the Lamb and some are inferior apostles of the churches. This is clearly not what Paul believed. He placed all apostles, whether called before or after the Ascension, on the same level. All apostles are apostles of Christ and are also apostles of the churches. In Paul's thinking there is no distinction. Dispensationalism and some Pentecostal teaching tries to discount and dismiss these apostles since they do not fit into their theological scheme. It would seem that it would be better to adjust our theology to the Word of God rather than trying to find a way to adjust the Scriptures.

These apostles are dismissed as inferior in some way because they are apostles of the churches, as if Paul's phrase creates a secondary class of apostles. The truth is that all apostles are apostles of the churches. Paul and Barnabas were apostles of the church at Antioch. The 12 Apostles were apostles of the Church at Jerusalem. We also note the positive language of Paul's description of all these apostles outside Jerusalem. They apparently were held in admiration by Paul, who described them as an "honor to Christ."

Isn't Paul's superiority to the other apostles proven by the fact that nearly half of the New Testament was written by him?

The fact that approximately half the New Testament was written by Paul is very persuasive evidence of the opinion of God about this man. As already noted, there are those who would elevate Paul and provide him a superior status based on his usefulness to God in writing so many New Testament books. However, Paul's superiority to other apostles is not proved on this basis. Peter wrote two books of the New Testament, and Luke also wrote two. Luke's books, his Gospel and Acts, are much longer and constitute a greater percentage of the New Testament than Peter's books. Yet, to conclude that Luke is equal or superior in authority to Peter on the basis of writing more New Testament verses is foolish. There is no New Testament reference that indicates that Luke was an apostle at all. In similar fashion, Barnabas has no New Testament book, yet Mark has one. To conclude from this that Barnabas was inferior to Mark is contrary to the testimony of Scripture, since it tells us that Barnabas was an apostle.

Likewise, the Old Testament prophetic books serve as an example. To conclude by the length of a particular prophetic book that a prophet was greater or lesser is not logical. In fact, some of the more powerful miracle-working prophets, such as Elijah and Elisha, wrote no Old Testament books at all.

Paul's usefulness to God as a writer of Scripture only testifies to his usefulness to God as a writer of Scripture, not to his superiority to other apostles called after the Ascension. Paul himself argues for his *equality* with other apostles, not superiority.

Perhaps turning to another example of this illogical thinking will help us to better understand Paul's role. For example, the descriptions of the Old Testament prophetic books as Major Prophets and Minor Prophets have caused some to erroneously conclude that is an evaluation of the greatness of the ministry of a particular prophet. It is actually only a grouping of books by their relative lengths. The Major Prophets are the longer books. The Minor Prophets are the shorter books. Some very outstanding prophets in the Scriptures wrote no books at all. In this list of great but non-writing prophets we must include Samuel, Elijah, Elisha, Nathan, and John the Baptist. There are many others. We cannot properly conclude that since these prophets did not write any books, they were somehow lesser prophets than Isaiah or Jeremiah. Such an argument is less than logical and certainly has no basis in Scripture. Yet this is the argument that is made for Paul's superiority over other apostles. It is an argument that Paul himself would never make.

God greatly used Paul, but he was only one of many apostolic servants of God revealed in the New Testament. The other apostles are not inferior because of Paul's usefulness as a writer of Scripture. His writings, however, provide us with most of our general information about the ministry of the apostle as well as a great deal of specific information about Paul's apostleship. For this we must give thanks to God for using His servant Paul so excellently as a writer of Scripture.

Does the existence of modern apostles mean that more Scripture is being written?

Absolutely not. The canon of Scripture is complete. The writing of Scripture is not an apostolic function and never was. If it were an apostolic function, then we should see all apostles in the New Testament writing Scripture. It is an obvious fact that only a few of the apostles revealed in Scripture wrote Scripture. In fact, some of the New Testament is written by persons whom the Bible does not call apostles, such as Mark and Luke. Hopefully, apostles in our day will be writing divinely inspired books, but they will not write Scripture. All revelation, written or otherwise, must be judged and humbly amended and corrected on the basis of Scripture. God help us to humble ourselves before His Word.

Aren't modern apostles less in authority and power than those of the first century?

No. If they are truly apostles, they are what the New Testament says about them. There are many who believe theoretically in a modern expression of apostles. However, many also teach a much-reduced role for the apostle than the Scriptures reveal. A good number of these teachers will cite bad experiences with those claiming to be apostles. Fear of extremes is not a good reason to deny or reduce this ministry against scriptural authority. Examining the Scriptures in detail is the answer. The false apostle can be separated easily from the true apostle if one knows what the Scriptures say about this ministry. We must be willing to apply the characteristics in Scripture to those who claim apostleship. This will reveal the true apostle from the false apostle and protect the Church.

Many of those who want to reduce the role of the apostle today borrow heavily from Dispensationalism while rejecting this doctrine's teaching on the Holy Spirit. Some popular Charismatic teachers build doctrinal systems built on "revelations" and "visitations" of the Lord that relegate apostles to a role reduced much from what the Scriptures reveal. Some of these doctrinal systems create classes of apostles and cause a reduced functioning of the apostle in this age. This teaching regarding apostolic classes comes, not from Scripture, but from the claims of a well-respected minister concerning a personal visitation from Jesus. This popular teacher says that Jesus taught him about the apostles for this age.

This is what this teacher says that Jesus taught him about apostles in summary form: All apostles are divided into four classes. Jesus Himself is the first class of apostles. The apostles of the Lamb are the second class of apostles. The rest of the apostles in the New Testament, including Paul, fall into a third class of apostles. The fourth class includes all modern apostles. Each class has less authority, anointing, and function than the previous class, according to this teaching.

There are several serious problems with this teaching when compared with the New Testament. There are several serious exceptions that invalidate this scheme. The first exception here is the ministry of James, the Lord's Brother. In this teaching James is in the third class of apostles, yet throughout the Book of Acts he is the authority at the church of Jerusalem. If this doctrinal scheme were correct, we would expect to see one of the apostles of the

Lamb (second class) exercising leadership. Instead we find one of the apostles who was called after the Ascension (third class) leading the church in Jerusalem. This is a contradiction to this doctrinal scheme. Apparently the church in Jerusalem was not aware of this teaching. Another contradiction is also readily apparent. To say that Paul was less in authority than the apostles of the Lamb is neither scriptural nor historical, yet in this scheme Paul is a third class apostle with less authority. There were certainly a few of the original 12 Apostles who were not as anointed as Paul or as useful to God. For instance, history and tradition records that the apostle Philip (not to be confused with the evangelist Philip) was rather undistinguished as an apostle. However, in this scheme, Philip would have been second class and Paul third class. This makes little sense, historically or logically.

The fourth class in this scheme includes all modern apostles. According to this teaching there are no apostles today who function in the same quality of anointing as the previous three classes. This teaching, in effect, says there are no apostles to whom the church must submit as they did in the New Testament era. It effectively negates God's Word about the authority of apostles by creating a different kind of apostle today, one who is not revealed in the Scriptures. The implication is that if this "low class" kind of apostle is not revealed, then we do not have to acknowledge what God's Word says about them since the instructions regarding apostles do not include them. This is a highly dangerous "revelation." This way of approaching the Scriptures will lead to disregard for the Scriptures and encourage rebellion against modern apostles. In fact, no resemblance can be found between the scriptural apostle and the kind of apostle that this scheme reveals.

This teaching places us in a kind of doctrinal limbo if we accept that God's Word for apostles as it is written is not true for today and must be modified by a revelation. We must then create a new doctrine to account for modern apostles which will be false and damage God's plan for the Church. It will also create problems for God's true apostles functioning on earth today. We cannot allow "visitations" or "revelations" that explain away God's Word and ultimately tell us we cannot trust what God has recorded. This is difficult to do when a teacher is highly respected, yet we must remain faithful to God's Word, not man's. What the Word of God says about apostles is true and remains true for today.

It is difficult to argue with "revelations" and "visitations" from the Lord Jesus Christ, particularly if the source is well-respected. However, if the outcome of the teaching ultimately says something that God's Word does not, or contradicts what God's Word says, then we must stand firm in the Scriptures. Anyone who says something on the basis of a personal revelation or visitation that God's Word does not, or attempts to adjust our understanding on that basis, has in effect placed his revelation or visitation above God's Word. Such a visitation or revelation then becomes the filter from which we come to understand (or rather, misunderstand) God's Word. Much cultic error has been perpetuated by such methods of interpretation. The great deceptions coming in the last days of this age will demand that we have a more careful and precise interpretation of Scriptures to avoid error.

Aren't apostles of today really missionaries?

Yes and no. It is more than possible that some modern missionaries are apostles, but it is clear that not all are apostles. Such persons are due our admiration for their commitment to the purposes of God, but most simply do not meet the majority of the criteria for apostolic ministry set forth in God's Word. Even though many might succeed in planting local churches, most operate with little evidence of a regular flow of miracles and healing, nor do they have independent confirmation of their calls as apostles.

Isn't apostleship over when the mission is completed?

No. Some doctrinal systems simply want to reduce the apostle to a temporary ministry of someone who has been sent with a message by God. They tell us that as soon as the message has been given then the calling of apostle is over. Although that is what the underlying Greek word *apostolos* means, this is not the full meaning of what the New Testament describes as apostles. In the New

Testament it was never a temporary ministry. Peter, Paul, and the others never ceased being apostles once they were sent by God.

It is inconsistent theology to state that this is a temporary ministry when it is listed with other permanent ministries. For instance, apostles are listed in First Corinthians 12 and Ephesians 4. Every other ministry listed there is of a permanent nature, so it is clearly inconsistent to say that the apostle is temporary. Although the Greek word is sometimes used for the temporary sending of an emissary, it is never used in that sense in reference to the 12 disciples or the other apostles of the early Church. Presentation of this idea is simply another modern attempt to reduce the apostle from his scriptural authority as revealed in the New Testament. This plays right into the enemy's desire to prevent apostles from assuming their God-given ministries.

Why are there so few apostles functioning today?

There are probably more apostles functioning and in preparation than any of us realize. However, they will remain relatively unknown or hidden until the proper time for revealing. Many barriers must be overcome before this ministry can be fully restored to the Church. There will be those who oppose restoration for a variety of reasons. There will be those who say, "The old wine is better," and choose to remain in their traditions. There will be those who will cling to the traditional bishop rather than make room for the apostle. There will be those who will be fearful of abuse and will look for abuses to justify their opinions. On the other hand, there will be many more who will hear what the Spirit is saying to the Church and will make room for this ministry. There will be many painful lessons for the Church until it learns to separate the true apostle from the false. Yet the Church has no option but to go through these things and expect full restoration of this ministry. The Bride must be prepared for the Bridegroom's coming; this will not happen until the apostle is fully restored in the Church.

Wasn't Peter the leader of all the apostles?

No. It doesn't appear that Peter ever held that particular distinction. He was definitely an important and influential apostle and considered by Paul to be a pillar of the church. However, careful study of the New Testament, particularly the Books of Acts and Galatians, reveals that James, the Lord's Brother, was the apparent leader of the church at Jerusalem and the other apostles located in that area.

Paul and Luke did not make any distinction between the earlier 12 Apostles and this later apostle, James, in their writings. From the testimony of the New Testament we don't know how James became the leader, but there is no question that he did. This reveals another flaw in Dispensational theology and in the teaching of those who would like to create classes of apostles. If Dispensational theology were correct about there being only 12 apostles, with Paul replacing Judas, it only follows that we should see one of those 12 men take over leadership in Jerusalem. It is apparent that this theology is not correct. All apostles, those called by Jesus prior to His crucifixion and resurrection and those called by the Holy Spirit after His Ascension, were considered equal in call, if not equal in authority. In Scripture an apostle called after the Ascension is in authority in Jerusalem even over the remaining apostles of the Lamb. For those who would like a theology of classes of apostles, James becomes a serious contradiction. James, the brother of Jesus, is not an apostle of the Lamb, yet these first apostles seem to have recognized his authority over them.

Is *apostolic succession* working in the ministry of apostles today?

There is no "apostolic succession" in the sense used by the Roman Catholic Church. However, there are young apostles being trained in the ministries of older apostles. It is possible that at the death of an older apostle God could set a younger apostle over his ministry. There might even be a time of transition where both function together in ministry. It is possible that this younger apostle might even be his son. In each case, the individual apostles and the elders must hear what the Spirit is saying to the Church.

How much danger is there in giving "kingly" authority to an apostle?

Certainly there are serious dangers if we are hasty or unwilling to seriously evaluate each apostolic claim. There is much more danger in failing to respond to what God reveals about apostles in His Word. In many churches, this kind of authority already functions with other titles, such as *bishop,* and without any evidence of apostleship. That is exceedingly dangerous. We must only allow those who have a tested ministry of apostleship to assume this kind of authority.

Beyond this, the Church must still be subject to the authority of Scripture. No apostle has any authority to invalidate or contradict Scripture. Should he ask someone to do something that is clearly forbidden by Scripture, that individual must obey God and not the apostle. He is not free to ask others to compromise their consciences or their integrity in any way. He must guard their freedom to find the will of God for themselves. He may only rule as a shepherd and by the consent of those who recognize his apostleship. His authority comes through God's revelation of his call to them. Should they not recognize his apostleship and submit themselves to it, he must still love them and minister to them at whatever level they will allow. His exercise of authority operates through a sincere love for the people God has given him and a desire to fulfill the will of God. He must not resort to fleshly methods of manipulation; rather he must patiently trust the Holy Spirit to instruct, correct, and lead the people of God. His leadership must be as a shepherd-king. Should he become a tyrant, the other apostles and elders of the Church must bring correction according to the pattern revealed in Scripture.

Doesn't an individual have to see the Lord like the original Twelve and Paul in order to be an apostle?

This idea comes from the Dispensational view of First Corinthians 9:1-2. There Paul makes this statement in argument that he should have the same rights as other apostles: "Am I not an apostle? Have I not seen the Lord?..."

The Dispensationalist, still holding to the doctrine of only 12 apostles and Paul replacing Judas, fits Paul into his scheme because of his vision of Christ on the road to Damascus. In their scheme Paul becomes an eyewitness like the other 12 Apostles. However, in the context of the passage, Paul is comparing himself with the 12 Apostles and defending his rights to be treated as an apostle (he also includes Barnabas). He is not making it a condition of apostleship to "see the Lord," but telling them that he is no less an apostle than the Twelve. We have no evidence that the other apostles named by Scripture saw the Lord physically or in a vision like Paul. Paul did not seem to consider it a requirement for their apostleship since he never mentions it again in his New Testament writings.

Why does my church have elected deacons leading it rather than appointed elders?

In those churches that have been dominated by Dispensational theology in the past, this kind of congregational church government is common. The theological reasoning from Dispensationalism is this: "Since the apostles and elders have passed away, all that leaves is the deacons, who were elected by the early Church." In other words, churches that have elected deacons who make decisions are a reflection of this faulty theology. These churches have a great many problems with disunity, church splits, and rebellion against pastoral authority as a result of failure to acknowledge what the Scriptures say about church government.

The original deacons were selected by the Church to wait on tables, not to make decisions about the spiritual direction of the Church. The elders continued to make these decisions and should do so today. This is not to say anything negative about individuals who serve as deacons in these churches. Generally speaking, they are elder material and extremely dedicated to the Lord. However, they generally have authority over the pastor or at least can make life difficult for him. Making matters worse, the congregation has authority over these elected deacons, and they must often bring important decisions before the congregation for a vote. This creates factions within churches over minor and major issues that the elders should have discussed privately, worked out and implemented without discussion with the congregation. In other words, in these churches the authority is upside down. Instead of the elders submitting to the pastor, the deacons to the elders, and the congregation to all the leadership, everything is reversed from the scriptural pattern.

In these situations the pastor really has limited authority to lead; he must seek permission to do his ministry from the deacons and, for anything serious, from the congregation. He cannot select other leaders of like spirit to serve as elders. He has little control over his own finances or his church's finances, and this can turn him into a hireling rather than a proper shepherd. Should his ministry offend anyone important, he may be in trouble and face a vote of the congregation. This kind of government turns many excellent leaders into politicians who are unable to speak anything that is controversial or corrective to an important member of the congregation. Wherever this kind of government has worked at all, it has been due to the strong Christian character and dedication of the people of God in these churches, not because it is a good form of church government. Many excellent servants of God have been dismissed from congregationally ruled churches because of the rebellion of a few members. In a proper arrangement of authority, it would be these rebellious members who would either submit, face discipline from the elders, or leave.

Are you (the author) an apostle?

No. It is very clear that at this stage of my life I am functioning as a teacher and learning to function as an "Elisha style" prophet. I do not have all the important characteristics I've listed in Chapter 3 that identify the apostle, nor do I expect to have them in the near future. Although I have had several prophecies from well-respected and mature men of God that have included the word *apostle*, I do not consider them as more than a "seed" that God may germinate in the unforeseen future. While I am clear that God has given me some limited vision about apostolic ministry, I am more than challenged with the things God has already put into my life and ministry. I do not desire or feel that I am prepared for the weight of responsibility and spiritual pressures that go along with the ministry of the apostle. I feel it is more than enough for me to be one "preparing the way" for those who are presently prepared to function as the Lord's apostle. God grant me the grace to do that well.

Bibliography

Duffield, Guy P., Editor, *Foundations of Pentecostal Theology*, Los Angeles, California: L.I.F.E. Bible College, 1983.

Gower, Ralph, *The New Manners and Customs of Bible Times*, Chicago, Illinois: Moody Press, 1987.

Lockyer, Herbert, *All the Apostles in the Bible*, Grand Rapids, Michigan: Zondervan Publishing House, 1970.

McDowell, *Evidence that Demands a Verdict, Vol. I*, San Bernadino, California: Here's Life Publishers, 1972.

The New Bible Commentary: Revised, Grand Rapids, Michigan: Eerdmans Publishing, 1910.

Robertson, Archibald Thomas, *Word Pictures in the New Testament, Vol. IV*, Grand Rapids, Michigan: Baker Book House, 1931.

Schaff, Phillip, *History of the Church, Vol. I*, Grand Rapids, Michigan: Eerdmans Publishing, 1910.

Vine, W.E., *The Expanded Vine's Expository Dictionary of New Testament Words*, Minneapolis, Minnesota: Bethany House Publishers, 1984.

Young, Robert, *Young's Analytical Concordance to the Bible*, 21st edition, Grand Rapids, Michigan: Eerdmans Publishing Company, 1970.

Additional single copies of this book at $9.95 plus $2.00 shipping can be obtained by writing:

All Nations Ministries
P.O. Box 8642
Norfolk, VA 23503-0642

Substantial discounts are available for groups, ministries, or bookstores for orders of five or more copies at $6.50 per copy and $1.00 shipping per copy. A listing of other materials from the author is also available on request.

All Nations Ministries
P.O. Box 8642
Norfolk, VA 23503-0642
1-804-853-8865
E mail: allntns@aol.com

All Nations Ministries
P.O. Box 8642
Norfolk, VA 23503-0642
1-804-853-8865
E mail: allntns@aol.com